Counter

Let's Get Blunt About Your Financial Affairs

A collection of the best blog posts from The Blunt Bean Counter

Mark Goodfield

Published and distributed by Blunt Bean Inc.

Email: bluntbeancounter@gmail.com

Web: www.thebluntbeancounter.com

Cover Design and Interior Images: Leah Vlemmiks

Page Composition and Proofreading: Lynda Kremer

ISBN: 1505226708

ISBN 13: 9781505226706

Library of Congress Control Number: 2014921459

CreateSpace Independent Publishing Platform

North Charleston, South Carolina

About Mark

Toronto native Mark Goodfield is no ordinary accountant. He's blunt, humorous and is known for telling his clients what they need to hear, which may be different than what they want to hear.

Mark honed his tax, business, and financial advisory skills over the past 25 years as a Chartered Professional Accountant (CPA). His experience is vast; he has worked for a Big 4 accounting firm, was a founding partner of Goodfield Girolametto (a small two-person partnership), and later on, assumed the leadership position of Taxation and Managing Partner of Cunningham LLP, a mid-sized, six-partner CPA firm in Toronto (subsequent to the initial printing of this book, Cunningham merged with a National firm).

Mark thrives on leveraging his financial acumen and business insights to help private corporations and their shareholders/owner-managers and senior officers achieve their goals. Sharing this knowledge and expertise beyond his current client base was the catalyst behind his popular financial blog, *The Blunt Bean Counter*.

Mark is a regular contributor to *The Globe and Mail* and has also been featured in the *Toronto Star*, *MoneySense*, CBC and other media outlets. Organizations such as the Canadian Bar Association, Law Society of Upper Canada, Canadian and Ontario Dental Associations, College of Veterinarians of Ontario, and Ontario Psychological Association have also tapped Mark as a presenter.

Mark gives back to the community through his involvement as a wish grantor for the Make-A-Wish Foundation. He is a former big brother for Big Brothers and Big Sisters of Toronto, and a former member of the Reena Foundation Investment Committee.

About The Blunt Bean Counter Blog

During the summer of 2009, the concepts of social media and content marketing were about as foreign to Mark and his fellow partners as GAAP is to non-Chartered Professional Accountants. In looking to better understand and embrace this new world of business communications, Mark engaged a marketing consultant to do a workshop that quickly turned into a hand slapping. "Modern marketing methods are here to stay," explained the presenter. The train had left while Mark and his fellow partners were still at the station. "Volunteers?" asked the marketer. In an effort to lead by example, Mark threw up his hand. This turned into a pivotal moment.

Mark, who had never even read a blog (except for an occasional investment or sports post), began reading and researching various financial blogs in Canada. While most of the bloggers were intelligent and well read, very few seemed to have or write about practical, "real life" client financial experiences. And, given the complexity of the *Income Tax Act*, few have dared to tackle those tough topics.

Before digging into his first post, Mark needed to name his new baby. He had often been told that his best and worst quality was being blunt. Accountants are often referred to somewhat derogatorily as "bean counters." Mark combined his cut-to-the-chase personality with his profession and *The Blunt Bean Counter* blog was born.

Mark's writing style, which is blunt, humorous and bit sarcastic at times, has filled a void for financial, business and tax insight that doesn't put readers to sleep. *The Blunt Bean Counter*, which has received over 1,600,000 page views since its inception in September 2010, has become one of Canada's top sites for discussions on income taxes, finance and money. Mark simplifies highly complex topics so his readers can understand and apply the knowledge to their personal and business situations. In staying true to form, he lightens his blunt technical talk with a twist of sarcasm and humor when possible.

In September 2014, after four years of hard work and some luck, Mark and *The Blunt Bean Counter* won the prestigious Plutus Award for the Best Tax Blog in Canada and the United States.

Contents

Disclaimer

This publication provides general information on various income tax issues and other financial matters. The information is not intended to constitute professional advice and may not be appropriate for a specific individual or fact situation, as each reader's personal financial situation is unique and fact specific.

Neither the author, Blunt Bean Inc. nor any firm with which the author is associated shall accept any liability in respect of any reliance on the information contained herein. Readers should always consult with their professional advisors in respect of their particular situation.

Introduction

Few of us like paying income tax; although I once had a client who told me at income tax time, to "Give unto Caesar, what is Caesar's" (a variation on the phrase in the *synoptic gospels*). Notwithstanding that client's philosophy, it has been my personal experience that most people feel Caesar takes too much in income taxes. Not to mention, the word "taxes" is generally associated with the word "audit" – *that makes for two very unpopular subjects.*

You would think writing a blog about taxes and other taboo financial topics such as "planning for your death" or "asking your parents for money" would be a recipe for disaster. Yet, my experience in writing *The Blunt Bean Counter* has been that people want to read and learn about these matters, as long as the writing is clear, plain and understandable. Since the blog's inception, I have attempted to do just that – *offer my tax, financial, and money-related expertise in a simplified format.* This is the book's premise.

In the pages to come, you will find information on a wide range of financial subjects such as planning for your estate, selecting your executor, tackling sticky family money issues, and lowering your tax bite. I selected the posts that "hit home" with my readers as evidenced by high web metrics and user-generated comments. These subjects are the most interesting, entertaining and/or applicable to common, real-life situations.

I hope you gain wisdom from this book and occasionally find a post or two that makes you laugh.

Chapter 1

The Lighter Side of Accounting

Are Accountants Really Boring?

The joke goes like this: "When does a person decide to become an accountant?" Drum roll please. The answer... "When they realize that they do not have the charisma to become an undertaker." Or how about this one? Question: "What does an accountant use for birth control?" Answer: "Their personality."

With a reputation like that, Flo Rida will not be penning any rap songs called *Wild Ones* featuring accountants. So are we accountants that boring or do we take an unfair rap?

Unfortunately, in general, I think the rap is probably warranted, although perception may be reality. How would we accountants be viewed if there had been a TV show called LA Accountant, instead of *LA Law*? Did you know John Grisham got his undergraduate degree in accounting? What if his books had been about accounting firms instead of law firms? Accountants would then be looked upon as cool dudes/dudettes with a conservative bent.

Is it nature or nurture? I think probably a combination of both. Many accountants by nature are cautious and conservative. Years of training to refine these character traits amplify the situation in non-professional environments. It would probably help if our dress style did not include pens hanging from our dress shirts, pencils behind our ears, or if we occasionally loosened our ties both literally and figuratively. I always had this underlying desire at a cocktail party full of accountants to run about the room and loosen all their ties.

When I am outed as an accountant, I always say I am a tax accountant or the managing partner to make my job sound sexier. Although my naturally-boring nature often gives me away, many of my other characteristics are non-accountant-like and I enjoy surprising people when they find out this blunt, sometimes arrogant, sometimes confrontational, and very occasionally humorous person is an accountant. My happiest social outings are not when a good-looking girl stares at me, but when someone says, "Wow, I would never have thought you to be an accountant."

So, are any of my kind not boring? For those of you old enough to remember *The Bob Newhart Show*, Bob Newhart, the namesake and star, was a former accountant. Now I am not sure Bob helps our cause. He was funny, but in a boring deadpan style, and he certainly was not stylish and definitely was no Chris Rock.

To my surprise I found a musician who started life as an accountant. You figure any musician would break the stereotype as they lead crazy drug-induced lifestyles. I found out Kenny G, a great saxophone player, is our exception. However, although Kenny is a great musician, I typically hear his music in my dentist's office and as far as I know, he did not trash too many hotel rooms.

I was about to give up when a beacon of light shone and led me to Paul Beeston. Finally, an accountant with attitude! Beeston, who was an accountant with Coopers and Lybrand, became the President and CEO of the Toronto Blue Jays and later the President and COO of Major League Baseball. Paul is a cigar-chomping, fun-loving, non-sock-wearing accountant. Yes, there is one out there.

There you have it, proof that there is an accountant out there who does not fit the stereotype. Anyway, if you ever meet me, I will be easy to spot. I am the outgoing accountant who will be looking down at your shoes instead of staring down at my own shoes.

Chapter 2

Executors - A Thankless Job
(except for the fees)

Speak to Your Executor – Surprise Only Works for Birthday Parties, Not Death

In this chapter I discuss many of the issues an executor may face. Being named an executor can be an overwhelming responsibility and as such, I feel you have an obligation to discuss a person's appointment as executor of your will with them. I will expand on this obligation further.

I have dealt with numerous estates where the executor(s) floundered, notwithstanding the fact they were provided direction. Where an executor flounders or spins their wheels, the ultimate beneficiaries suffer in two ways: (1) their financial entitlement is often delayed months, if not years; and (2) that entitlement may be reduced because of poor investment decisions or non-decisions made by the executor.

Where an executor is in over their head, I place the blame solely upon the deceased. Many people do not take the proper amount of time to consider the personal characteristics of the executor they have selected. What I consider most objectionable is that many people never provide the executor with the courtesy of notice of their potential appointment. In addition, many do not even attempt to meet with their executors to discuss their potential duties and whether they feel comfortable being named as an executor.

I consider the personal characteristics of a potential executor to be of the utmost of importance. I would suggest a potential executor should: (1) have some financial acumen; (2) not stress easily; and (3) be somewhat anal.

At the risk of stereotyping, I have been involved with a couple executors who were more artistic than financial in nature and they were overwhelmed by the position. In my opinion, the reason they were overwhelmed was that their personal characteristics were the complete polar opposite of the characteristics I recommend an executor possess. Years ago I had a very high-strung person named as the executor of an estate, and they essentially shut down for over a year due to the stress of the job and the estate sat in limbo.

This is not to suggest that an artistic person cannot be an executor or a co-executor with a financial person, but I would suggest that before naming such a person, you sit down and explain the duties of an executor to ensure that they feel they can handle the job.

In many cases, people name their children as executors. I have no problem with doing such; however, you must look at each child's personal characteristics and the sibling dynamic to determine whether they can handle the job as a group or whether you have to name only one or two of your children as executors. I think many people would name executors from outside the family if the potential executor fees did not approach up to 5% of the estate; however, in some cases, paying the executor fee is worth the independence gained by having an arm's length person administer the estate, despite the associated fees.

So what are the key takeaways? (1) You must seriously consider your selection of an executor and their personal characteristics; and (2) once you have made your selection, I would strongly suggest you discuss their appointment with them.

You Have Been Named an Executor, Now What?

So, John Stiff dies and you are named as an executor. What duties and responsibilities will you have? Immediately you may be charged with organizing the funeral, but in many cases, the immediate family will handle those arrangements, assuming there is an immediate family in town. What's next? Well, a lot of work and frustration dealing with financial institutions, the family members and the beneficiaries.

Below is a laundry list of many of the duties and responsibilities you will have as an executor:

- Your first duty is to participate in a game of hide and seek to find the will and safety deposit box key(s). If you are lucky, someone can tell you who Mr. Stiff's lawyer was and, if you can find him or her, you can get a copy of the will. Many people leave their will in their safety deposit box; you may need to find the safety deposit key first, so you can open the safety deposit box to access the will.

- You will then need to meet with the lawyer to coordinate responsibilities and understand your fiduciary duties from a legal perspective. The lawyer will also provide guidance with respect to obtaining the Letters Probate (a very important step in Ontario and most other provinces).

- You will then want to arrange a meeting with Mr. Stiff's accountant (if he had one) to determine whether you will need his/her help in the administration of the estate or, at a minimum, for filing the required income tax returns. If the deceased does not have an accountant, you will probably want to engage one.

- Next up may be attending the lawyer's office for the reading of the will; however, this is not always necessary and is probably more of a "Hollywood creation" than a reality.

- You will then want to notify all beneficiaries of the will of their entitlement and collect their personal information (address, social insurance number, etc).

- You will then start the laborious process of trying to piece together the deceased's assets and liabilities (see Chapter 3 *Where Are the Assets?* for a suggestion on how to make this task easy for your executor).

- The next task can sometimes prove to be extremely interesting. It is time to open the safety deposit box at the bank. I say "extremely interesting" because what if you find significant cash? If you do, you then have your first dilemma; is this cash unreported, and what is your duty in that case?

- It is strongly suggested that you attend the review of the contents of the safety deposit box with another executor. A bank representative will open the box for you and you need to make a list on the spot of the box's contents, which must then be signed by all present.

- While you are at the bank opening the safety deposit box, you will want to meet with a bank representative to open an estate bank account and find out what expenses the bank will let you pay from that account (assuming there are sufficient funds) until you obtain probate. Most banks will allow funds to be withdrawn from the deceased's bank account to pay for the funeral expenses and the actual probate fees. However, they can be very restrictive initially and each bank has its own set of rules.

- As soon as possible you will want to change Mr. Stiff's mailing address to your address and cancel credit cards, utilities, newspapers, fitness clubs, etc.

- As soon as you have a handle on the assets and liabilities of the estate, you will want to file for Letters Probate, as moving forward without probate is next to impossible in most cases.

- You will need to advise the various institutions of the passing of Mr. Stiff and find out which documents will be required to access the funds they have on hand. In one estate I had about ten different institutions to deal with and I swear not one seemed to have the exact same informational requirements as another.

- If there is insurance, you will need to file claims and make claims for things such as the Canada Pension Plan ("CPP") benefit.

- You will need to advertise in certain legal publications or newspapers to ensure there are no unknown creditors; your lawyer will advise what is necessary.

- It is important that you either have the accountant track all monies flowing in and out of the estate or you do it yourself in an accounting program or Excel. You may need to engage someone to summarize this information in a format acceptable to the courts if a "Passing of Accounts" is required in your province to finalize the estate.

- You will also need to arrange for the re-investment of funds with the various investment advisors until the funds can be paid out. For real estate you will need to ensure supervision and/or management of any property and ensure insurance is renewed until the properties are sold.

- A sometimes troublesome issue is family members taking items, whether for sentimental value or for other reasons. They must be made to understand that all items must be allocated and nothing can be taken.

- You will need to arrange with the accountant to file a "T1 Terminal Return" covering the period from January 1st to the date of death. Consider whether a special return for "Rights or Things" should be filed. You may also be required to file an "Executor's Year" tax return for the period from the date of death to the one year anniversary of Mr. Stiff's death. Once all the assets have been collected and the tax returns filed, you will need to obtain a clearance certificate to absolve yourself of any responsibility for the estate and create a plan of distribution for the remaining assets (you may have paid out interim distributions during the year).

The above is just a brief list of some of the more important duties of an executor. For the sake of brevity I have ignored many others.

The job of an executor is demanding and draining. Should you wish to take executor fees for your efforts, there is a standard schedule for fees in most provinces. For example in Ontario, the fee is 2.5% of the receipts of the estate and 2.5% of the disbursements of the estate.

Finally, it is important to note that executor fees are taxable as the taxman gets you coming, going, and even administering the going.

Make Things Easier for Your Family and Executor – Designate Personal Effects in Your Will

In March of 2011, I wrote a post titled *Personal Use Property – Taxable Even If the Picasso Walks out the Door* (see Chapter 6). I discussed the taxation of personal use property and noted how many parents often neglect to deal with their art, jewelry, collectibles, and sentimental personal effects in their wills. These omissions may be either inadvertent, or on purpose, to avoid paying income tax and/or probate tax on the personal use property. The ramifications of this neglect are potentially twofold:

1. Parents, who take a leap of faith believing that their children will sort out the ownership of these assets in a detached and non-emotional manner, may be creating unnecessary dissension amongst their children.

2. Parents put their executor(s), who are often one or more of their children, in a precarious position with respect to their liability for probate and income tax of the estate.

Ensuring an Orderly Distribution of Personal Property

Lynne Butler, an estate lawyer and the writer behind the excellent blog *Estate Law Canada*, had this to say about personal effects: "My experience over the years has been that more estate fights happen over personal items of the deceased than happen over money. Sure we all like money but it's the personal items that have the sentimental value."[1]

So how can parents mitigate the potential for a family fight? In three words: inventory and document. Parents need to undertake a detailed review of all personal items from art and antiques to jewelry to great grandma's tea set and ensure these items are reflected in their wills. Where there are significant variations in value for items such as art, antiques and jewelry, parents can choose to ignore the valuation issue and just leave those personal items to the child they wish. The other option they have is to equalize these disparities in value in their will through cash or other means. For less valuable items with sentimental value, the will should be as detailed as possible. The key is to ensure you minimize the amount of unallocated personal effects not included in your will.

Personal Effects Not Listed in the Will

Some provinces, such as Ontario, are concerned there has been significant probate tax leakage in the last few years, and they are attempting to plug the leakage. Executors will potentially have liability and penalty concerns. Parents in all provinces should understand that by not fully documenting their personal effects in their wills, they may be putting their executor or co-executors in an untenable position.

So what do executor or co-executors do when the last surviving parent passes away and they have not addressed the distribution of all their personal effects in their will? How do executors ensure siblings or relatives of the deceased don't help themselves to these personal assets, as has been known to occur on more than one occasion, and how do they distribute these assets without creating a family war?

Here are some suggestions:

1. As soon as possible, change the locks on the deceased's home and ensure all assets are secured in the home. Valuable assets should be put into the deceased's safety deposit box, if the bank allows such, or put into a new estate safety deposit box.

2. Call a meeting of the beneficiaries and make it clear to them that they are not to remove any assets from the home and set out your intended plan of distribution of the personal effects.

3. Inventory and catalog all assets.

4. Get rid of the "junk". We all accumulate old clothes, furniture etc. Weed out the crap and inform the beneficiaries they should see if there is anything they want, or these effects will be donated or removed by a junk removal service.

5. After you have had time to ensure everything has been accounted for and the estate is starting to move forward, distribute the assets that were noted in the will in accordance with the deceased's instructions.

6. Lastly, comes the hardest part. How do you distribute the deceased's personal effects that have not been itemized in their will? I have read, heard or seen the following possibilities:

   a) For large valuable assets, attach values and attempt to distribute proportionately, if the assets allow for proportional distribution. First pick could be determined by draw and the person choosing last would then pick first the second time around. If the assets are disproportional, you can auction off the assets to the beneficiaries for a proposed value. If the value received by one beneficiary exceeds that of another beneficiary, the excess value received can be equalized with cash they have received from the estate or their own funds.

   b) For less valuable assets and sentimental assets, see if you can work something out with the family and/or beneficiaries. The beneficiaries can rank the assets one to ten and the assets are then allocated to the beneficiary with the highest ranking of each asset. Alternatively, a lottery can be used or any other method the beneficiaries can agree upon. You just want to distribute assets as fairly as possible while trying to minimize any issues between the beneficiaries.

Parents need to be cognizant of the precarious position they may leave their executor(s) in when they do not itemize and allocate as many of their personal effects as possible in their will. For personal items not listed in the will, executor(s) need to secure, inventory, and organize these personal effects and create a plan for the distribution of such assets.

---

1   Butler, Lynne. "How to Make a Plan for Your Personal Effects." Estate Law Canada. May 10, 2011.

Chapter 3

Inheritances, Wills and Estates – Love, Money and Greed

Estate Planning – Taking It to the Grave or Leaving It All to Your Kids?

I am often engaged to provide estate planning. Many people born to the "silent generation [1925-1945]" have amassed great wealth; a 2006 Decima Research study estimated that over one trillion dollars in wealth could be transferred between 2006-2026[1]. After 25 years of discussions regarding the distribution of wealth, it is my opinion that where an estate will clearly have excess funds when the parents pass away, consideration should be given to transferring that wealth in partial gifts during a parent's lifetime.

I have observed that people form four distinct groups: those that will take their wealth to their grave (or leave it to their pet Chihuahua); those that will distribute their wealth only upon their death; those that may not be able to afford their grave (as they give and give to their children); and the most common, the middle ground of the extremes, those who are willing to distribute their wealth, but may harbour concerns that their wealth will be "blown" or lead to unmotivated children.

Below I discuss these four groups with the understanding that my opinions may be diametrically opposed to yours.

For those who wish to take their wealth to the grave, there is often a deep-rooted family issue, and the chill in the room makes it very clear that advisors should stay clear of delving into these family issues.

In the case of those who wish to distribute their wealth upon their death, the issue is typically philosophical. That is, one or both of the parents feel that their children need to make their own way in the world, and that leaving them money during their lifetime will do their children a disservice or destroy their moral compass. This is a touchy area, but I often suggest that if the parents feel their children are well-adjusted, they should consider providing partial inheritances. A partial inheritance can facilitate a child's dream, such as climbing Mount Kilimanjaro while the child is physically able, or assisting with the down payment on a cottage. The selling point on partial distributions is that the parents can share vicariously in the joy of the experience they facilitate.

In the third situation, the parents spend every spare nickel on their children's private school, dance lessons, hockey teams, etc., while younger and then assist in buying houses, cars, etc., when they are older, to the detriment of their own retirement (let alone the distribution of their wealth). In these cases I suggest the parents pare back the funds they spend on their children and/or make the children contribute to their own activities. It is imperative the parents impart upon their children that they are not an ATM and that there are family budgetary limits to be adhered to, which is often easier said than done.

The majority of families fall into the last category. They are willing to distribute their "excess" wealth while alive, but in many cases harbour concerns their wealth will be "blown" or lead to unmotivated children. Dr. Lee Hausner, an advisor to some of the wealthiest families in the United States, suggests in some of her various articles that parents do not transfer money during career-building years so the children learn to be productive members of society. Children should be taught they have choices to make (e.g. distribute money for one thing they want, but not three things they want), and they should learn to be philanthropic amongst other things.[2] I think this advice stands on its own whether you are one of the wealthiest families in the United States or just a family that has been lucky enough to accumulate more assets than you will ever require.

How one distributes their wealth is an extremely private issue and each individual has their own thoughts and reasons for their actions. However, in my opinion, where the parents have the financial wherewithal, they should consider making at least partial gifts during their lifetime, while heeding Dr. Hausner's advice.

Is It Morbid or Realistic to Plan for an Inheritance?

I have written various articles on estate planning and inheritances in which I discuss whether parents should distribute future inheritances in part or in whole while they are alive.

These articles elicited a wide range of opinions and comments that I found fascinating. Some people believe they are better off because their parents made them work for everything, and they don't want any financial assistance from their parents either during their life or after they pass away. Others state that as long as parents are careful to ensure they don't destroy their children's motivation, partial inheritances make sense. Finally, others say they have been sickened as they observe children waiting at a parent's deathbed salivating at the thought of their inheritance.

All this leads me to another very touchy subject; should a child (let's assume the child is at least 40 years old) plan their own financial future based on a known or presumed inheritance? To add some perspective to this issue, it is interesting to note that a recent survey by the *Investors Group* states that 53% of Canadians are expecting an inheritance, with over 57% of those expecting an inheritance greater than $100,000.[3]

Inheritances can be categorized as either known or presumed inheritances. An inheritance would be categorized as known when a parent has discussed the contents of their will with their children, or at least made known their intentions. In these cases, while the certainty of the inheritance in known, the quantum is subject to the vagaries of the parent(s)' health, the parent(s)' lifestyle, the income taxes due on the death of the last-to-survive parent and the economic conditions of the day. (Speaking of discussing the will with your children, it is very interesting to note that my post *One Big Happy Family – Until We Discuss the Will*, which had limited initial traction, is now by far the most read post I have ever written. This post follows later in this chapter.)

An inheritance may be presumed where the financial circumstances of the family are obvious. A child cannot help but observe that the house their parents purchased 30 or 40 years ago for $25,000 is now worth $800,000 to $1,000,000, or that the cottage their family bought for $100,000 many years ago can be subdivided and is now worth $700,000.

Many average Canadian families have amassed significant net worth just by virtue of the gains on their real estate purchases. These families would not be considered wealthy based on lifestyle or income level, yet their legacy can have a significant impact upon their children. Inheritances are not only an issue for wealthy families.

I think most people will agree that where an inheritance will be so substantial that it will be life changing, parents need to downplay the inheritance issue and/or manage the inheritance by providing partial gifts during their lifetime. Rarely can a child become aware of a life-changing inheritance without losing motivation and experiencing a change in their philosophical outlook on life.

Although life-changing inheritances are rare, life-"affecting" inheritances are not. So, should children change how they live and how they plan for the future based on a known or presumed future inheritance? In my opinion, if the inheritance is known and will be substantial enough to alter a child's current or future living standard, the answer is a lukewarm yes, subject to the various caveats I discuss below.

I think it is nonsensical to ignore reality where a known inheritance has the attributes noted above and it should be considered as part of your future financial plan. However, I would discount the amount used for planning purposes significantly, to account for inherent risks.

Those risks include the longevity of a parent, economic downturns that reduce your parents' yearly income stream, potential medical costs, and finally, the ultimate risk one takes in planning for an inheritance: the risk of somehow falling out of favour and being removed from your parent(s)' will.

Where there is a presumed inheritance, I would suggest you need to be ultra conservative if you want to plan for the inheritance, since not only are you guessing at the inheritance amount, but you face an additional risk that your parents may have offsetting liabilities such as a mortgage or line of credit of which you are unaware.

So what do the experts have to say on this matter? In the press release for the *Investors Group* survey, Christine Van Cauwenberghe, Director, Tax and Estate Planning, says that "Knowing the dollars and cents behind your inheritance can have an impact on your financial plans. ... It is smart to know what you can expect so you can plan accordingly and family dialogue is a good place to start."[4]

I think Christine's comments clearly point out the conundrum here, for which there is no black and white answer. It is probably unwise to ignore a known potential inheritance, but because the final inheritance is subject to so many variables, you must risk assess that inheritance and discount its quantum by a significant amount, such that your planning becomes a paradoxical situation.

But what if you see no risk in your parents' financial situation deteriorating and you feel you will never be removed from the will, how can your financial planning be affected? For argument's sake, let's say your inheritance will be large enough to affect your future planning, but not large enough to affect your motivation or change your lifestyle.

The most obvious change to your financial plan may be to underfund your Registered Retirement Savings Plan ("RRSP"). Most Canadians struggle to make yearly RRSP contributions. They live in mortal fear that they will not have enough money to live the retirement they envision. But, if you know your parent(s) have enough funds to live out their life/lives comfortably, and say your inheritance will be in the $300,000 to $500,000 range, do you need to make your maximum RRSP contribution each year?

Other planning issues include whether you should purchase a home out of your price range or underfund your children's education fund, knowing that you will receive an inheritance to pay off the mortgage or to pay off any education-related loans. Alternatively, you may overfund your child's education by sending them to a private school you would never have considered without knowledge or presumption of a future inheritance.

How you deal with debt could also be affected. If you have debt, should you just limit it to a manageable level and not concern yourself with paying it down? Or alternatively, should you pay it off because you can reallocate funds once committed to your RRSP, Tax-Free Savings Account ("TFSA") or Registered Education Savings Plan ("RESP"), knowing your inheritance will cover your RRSP, TFSA, or RESP?

We have all heard about the huge debt level many Canadians are carrying. One wonders if, at least subconsciously, some of this debt level is being carried because people know they have an inheritance coming, and that their debt load will be insignificant once they receive their inheritance.

So, have I seen people bank on an inheritance? Yes. To date, where I have observed such behaviour, the inheritances have come as expected. However, these cases may not be predictive of future cases.

Is it morbid to plan for an inheritance? Clearly, it is. Would most people rather have their parents instead of the inheritance? Yes. This topic is a very touchy subject and an extremely slippery slope, but to ignore the existence of a significant future inheritance that would impact upon your personal financial situation may be nonsensical. However, if your financial planning takes into account a future inheritance, you should ensure you have discounted that amount to cover the various risks and variables that could curtail your inheritance and be extremely conservative in your planning.

Inheriting Money – Are You a Loving Child, a Waiter or a Hoverer?

Over the last 25 years, I have dealt with the tax, financial, and psychological issues surrounding numerous client estates. I have also observed the behaviors and actions of those who stand to inherit money from their parents, and I have found their behavior to be anywhere from fascinating to sickening.

I have found people who will inherit money fall into four groups:

1. The Loving Child
2. The Pragmatic Loving Child
3. The Waiters
4. The Hoverers

The Loving Child

For this group, their parents come first and money is secondary. Typically, these children are very close to their parents throughout their lives and call and see them on a consistent basis (often weekly, or even daily). They have always helped their parents with their medical needs or, in some cases, with their financial needs without giving it a second thought because their parents are, well, their parents. This group would tell you they would give back any inheritance if it allowed them another day to be with their parents, and would consider it blasphemy to plan for an inheritance.

The Pragmatic Loving Child

This group is a subset of group 1. These children love their parents and just want their parents to enjoy their lives, even if it means that they spend the children's inheritance. Children in this group may consider the reality that they will likely receive an inheritance. Even so, they do not want to take it into account in their planning and it is only at the insistence of an accountant or financial planner that they would even consider such.

The Waiters

I am not sure who coined this term, but I have seen it used many times. Waiters are described as children waiting for their parents to die, so that they can benefit from their parents' assets. Waiters are considered to have a warped sense of entitlement to their parents' money. I have observed several Waiters over the years, some of whom went into debt to live a lifestyle based on an assumed inheritance. In my limited sample size, the children have always received their inheritances. However, one day I would love to see the face of a Waiter when a lawyer informs them their parent decided to leave everything to charity instead of them.

The Hoverers

Hoverers are an even lower species than the Waiters. These children often pay little or no attention to their parents throughout their lives, but when their parents get sick or older, they start hovering around. Several years ago, one of my clients was very sick and was expected to pass away any day. When I received a call from one of his children, I assumed the call was going to be the bad news that my client had passed away and the child was going to provide me the details of the funeral. The call was indeed to tell me their parent had passed away, but they were not calling to tell me about the funeral arrangements; their question to me was when could they start accessing their inheritance? I just felt sick to my stomach.

Don't ask me why I decided to write about this topic. I guess, as I have stated many times in my blog, I am just fascinated by how money affects people's behavior. Thankfully, most people fall into the first two groups. If you are a Waiter or Hoverer, consider taking a good look at yourself in the mirror.

Where Are the Assets?

If you died tomorrow, would your family and advisors know where your assets are and what assets you owned?

I would suggest the answer in 50% or more cases would be a resounding no.

If you have answered no, take this one step further; consider the havoc you will cause your family and executors. They will be distressed having to deal with your passing, and now you are compounding their stress by forcing them to deal with an estate when they have no clue what assets you own, what debts you have outstanding, or where the assets are held. Most likely they will not have a duplicate safety deposit key or even know where your safety deposit box(es) is/are.

Whether you are just negligent or lazy, your actions are selfish and you should immediately take steps to rectify the situation.

All this can be averted very simply. Take a weekend and complete a personal information checklist and then put a reminder in your Blackberry, iPhone or Outlook calendar to review this checklist each year to ensure there are no changes.

Once completed, make at least three copies of your checklist and provide a copy to your spouse and one to either your accountant, lawyer, or trusted third party. Then put the final copy in your safety deposit box and ensure either your spouse or another person is aware of the location of the safety deposit box and the key.

One Big Happy Family – Until We Discuss the Will

A question many parents ponder is should they have a family meeting to discuss their will with their children?

When there is a "black sheep" child in the family, or a child who is not treated equally in the will, I expect that a family meeting would likely be a disaster. But what about a meeting in situations when the children are treated somewhat equally? There is no right or wrong answer, but I think a family meeting is wise. Any meeting of this type can turn ugly because of money issues, but more likely, any ugliness will be the result of historical family jealousies or resentment over some prior issue or treatment. Nevertheless, if you feel you can navigate the minefields noted above, the family meeting can be very effective and useful.

The family meeting could be used to deal with or clarify several different types of issues. For example:

1. *Possible perceived inequalities:* The meeting could be used to explain why you have left your Picasso to your daughter instead of your son so that he doesn't feel slighted when the will is read. This discussion could involve explaining that since your daughter studied art history at university, you feel she would appreciate the Picasso; however, since it is worth $500,000, you have left your son $500,000 of stock to equalize (or you have not tried to equalize, you can explain why face-to-face). Also, where you have left more money to one child (perhaps they make less money than the other children), you can use the meeting to explain why and explain that it has nothing to do with loving that child more, you are just helping them since they have not been as fortunate as the other siblings.

2. *Determine wants and needs of the beneficiaries:* Many families have second properties such as cottages or ski chalets. Some

children may have attachments to these properties while others may not, or maybe you are not sure whether any child would want to take over the property when you pass. A meeting provides the opportunity to raise the issue for your children to decide among themselves if they will want to sell the property, share the use, or have one child inherit the property. This issue may be best discussed prior to a will being finalized.

3. *Deciding on an executor:* Most children have no idea of the responsibilities and the burden of being named an executor of the will. You can broach this topic at the meeting to explain the duties of the executor and determine if the children or child you wish to be an executor(s) are/is willing to undertake the position.

4. *Full disclosure:* Finally, depending how open you wish the meeting to be, you can provide a current list of assets to your children so they know what assets you own and where they are held. You should also provide such a list to your accountant or lawyer, or put such a list in your safety deposit box, but you must ensure such a document exists and someone knows where it is.

The decision to have a family meeting to explain your estate planning while alive and in good mental and physical health is a complex decision based on past family history and relationships. However, if you feel the meeting can be held without creating a "civil war," it gives you a great chance to explain your estate planning and to get everyone onside.

Memory Overload, Alzheimer's, and Death in the Digital World

About a year and a half ago, my wife (who is an avid reader), kept telling me about a book she was reading titled *Still Alice* by Lisa Genova (now a movie starring Julianne Moore). Eventually I became so intrigued, I read the book. This best-selling novel tracks the tragic decline of a brilliant 50-year-old woman suffering from the early onset of Alzheimer's, the impact on her family, and the decisions she makes once she accepts the reality of what is happening to her. If you have not read the book, I suggest you read it. It is both disturbing and thought-provoking.

After reading the book, I recommended it to a service provider of mine. This person read the book and one day we discussed it. Our discussion veered off onto how hard it is for a person with full capacity to remember all the electronic passwords we are required to set up in this day and age (assuming you do not use the same password for all your financial and social sites, which is frowned upon by most computer security experts). As our discussion progressed, we considered the nightmare it would be to deal with all the electronic banking, billing, etc., if god forbid we developed Alzheimer's as Alice did in the book.

The discussion took an unexpectedly darker turn, when this person told me that they recently had a huge issue when a family member passed away unexpectedly at a fairly young age, and since that person was computer literate, much of their world was digital, but no one had a clue as to their electronic passwords.

The above discussion revealed three different scenarios that can arise in this electronic and digital era:

    1. You have full capacity but just cannot remember all your passwords.

2. Your capacity begins to diminish, whether through Alzheimer's or just old age.

3. You or a family member passes away, and you or a family member as executors must deal with electronic and digital records for which you have no access and whose existence you may not even be aware of.

Personally, I have completed an information checklist so my wife is aware of the assets we have. I have also made sure she is aware of our more important financial passwords. As someone who is by no means a computer whiz, I surfed the web to see what others were recommending or suggesting in regard to these various digital issues.

Use an Electronic Password Manager

There are a number of services that allow you to enter all your passwords into a single database and lock them up with a master electronic key. You (or your agent) only need to remember one password to access the list.

You may also wish to make a backup onto a USB flash drive, which becomes a mini encrypted vault with a password of its own. The drawback here is you must find someplace secure to store it.

Using either a USB flash drive or password service addresses situation 1, where you have full mental capacity, but are just suffering from password overload.

Rely on a Digital Gatekeeper

One way around the mental capacity issue is to store the digital data that you enter and release it according to your instructions.

Some firms that have come onto the scene that help individuals protect and transfer their digital assets; iCroak, Entrustet and Legacy Locker.

I have no recommendation on whether you should use these sites or not; I am just making you aware of their existence.

In any event, these sites or others that are developed in the future (I would suggest eventually the large trust companies will develop something similar) are probably the wave of the future and would address situation 2 and 3.

Old School Solutions

Finally, there are the tried and true "old school" solutions of using a notebook, or a safe, or lock box.

I would suggest that both these solutions are probably used in some manner by many people, but are not exactly state-of-the-art, and have inherent security issues.

As I stated earlier, I am far from a computer security whiz. The intention is to bring attention to the various electronic and digital issues noted above, and to make sure if you have not already addressed these issues in some manner, you consider doing such.

Stress-Testing Your Spouse's Financial Readiness If You Were to Die Suddenly

I have written about several morbid estate planning topics; however, I think this article easily ranks as #1 on the morbidity scale.

I will have the impertinence to suggest that you should stress-test how financially and organizationally ready your spouse would be should you die suddenly, or vice versa. Essentially, I am telling you to take a financial and organizational walk through your death.

As I don't want to be known as Morbid Mark, I am going to provide a side benefit of undertaking this morbid task. Girls, instead of the usual headache excuse, tell your guy "Sure, but first let's stress-test your death." I guarantee you will have the night off. Guys, if your wife is taking you to the ballet, just before you are about to leave, tell her you just want to financially stress-test her death and I don't think you will have to attend *The Nutcracker*.

Seriously though, even with today's modern families where both spouses often have some level of financial acumen, most families really give little thought to what would happen if, god forbid, one of them passed away unexpectedly.

It is important to understand that this article is not intended just for older readers, but for anyone married or in a common-law relationship, no matter their age. A 40-year-old can get hit by a car anytime, just as much as an elderly person can pass away due to old age. The idea for this article came about because I realized if I passed away suddenly, I had only partially provided my wife a financial road map of our assets, insurance policies, etc. Why I am even cognizant of such a morbid concern is because my father passed away suddenly 25 years ago, and if I were not an accountant, my mother would have been overwhelmed trying to find insurance policies, bank accounts and various other investments at a time of intense grief and shock.

Some of the issues that need to be stress-tested:

1. If you have pre-paid your funeral or have certain wishes, ensure your spouse is aware of where this information is located.

2. Does your spouse know where to find a copy of and/or the lawyer who drafted your will? More importantly, is your will up to date? If you own your own company, do you have two wills?

3. Do you have a folder for all your insurance policies? Does your spouse know where it's located? While in good health, you should prepare a summary of all insurance policies you have on an Excel spreadsheet; list the policy number, the insurance company, the type of insurance as well as the value of the insurance, and staple it to the front of your insurance folder. You may also want to create a special password-protected file (let's call it the "Information Folder" for lack of a better name) on your spouse's computer that contains this summary information.

4. Do you have a list of the assets you own and where they are located? As I discussed in *Where Are the Assets?*, you should complete and update yearly a basic information checklist. Again, I suggest a PDF placed in your Information Folder.

5. As I discussed in *Memory Overload, Alzheimer's, and Death in the Digital World*, the use of multiple passwords is so prevalent that you should consider making a list of your key passwords for your spouse, that again is either put into the Information Folder or another more secure location. The objective of this exercise is to ensure your spouse will not be locked out of your various financial accounts because he/she does not know the passwords.

6. Do you have a contact list for your spouse with the phone numbers and contact information of your accountant, lawyer and financial advisor? Again, consider creating a PDF and putting it in the Information File. You should also introduce your spouse to these key service providers so they will have a familiarity with them.

7. Consider any accounts, safety deposit boxes, etc., your spouse may not be aware of. There are various reasons one spouse does not make another spouse aware of these items, however, the reason for their existence is not relevant here; what is important is that you somehow ensure that someone will become aware of the existence of these accounts or safety deposit boxes if you die.

The above list is far from comprehensive. However, the intention was not completeness, but to get you to take a step back and consider the unthinkable and whether or not you have prepared the proper trail to allow your grieving spouse to move forward financially with the least amount of stress. I know this is morbid and people tend to procrastinate or ignore anything related to death, but look at this as selfless instead of morbid and maybe you will be moved to act.

---

1 The Canadian Inheritance Study, Decima Research. 2006.

2 Hausner, Lee. *Children of Paradise: Successful Parenting for Prosperous Families.* Los Angeles: Tarcher, 1990.

3 Investors Group. "Trillion Dollar Wealth Transfer – Myth or Reality?" Investors Group. February 8, 2012.

4 Ibid.

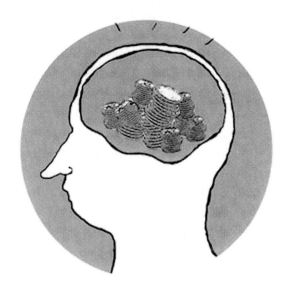

Chapter 4

The Psychology of Money - Is it Everything?

Are Money and Success the Same Thing? – Part 1

The *Toronto Star* used to run a weekly feature called *Fame and Fortune*, where famous people discussed various financial lessons they had learned and provided financial advice. The last question was always "Are money and success the same thing?" In the columns I read, I do not ever recall a featured guest answering yes to this question. Yet, the fact that the question is asked insinuates that some people feel the answer is yes. I would further suggest that we all have met people who we think would answer yes to this question (or should answer yes), based on their actions.

In my opinion, the brevity of the *Fame and Fortune* column forced a cliché answer from most of the guests. The guests typically said things such as "money is fleeting," or "money does not buy love," or "people should not be defined by their money". However, this simple question is actually very complex when you peel back the layers. Success can be defined and interpreted in so many ways. I believe that money and success are not one and the same, but are so closely intertwined in some circumstances, that money may allow you to buy certain variations of success, while in other situations it can derail success.

What is Success?

The definition of success is elusive. If you asked 100 people, you would probably get 100 different answers as to how they define success. So I turned to some famous and less-famous people, and their definitions and interpretations of success (and money) are as follows:

John Wooden, considered by many as the greatest basketball coach ever, had this definition: "Success is peace of mind, which is a direct result of self-satisfaction in knowing you made the effort to do your best to become the best that you are capable of becoming."[1]

Another interpretation of money and success is provided by American author and motivational speaker Wayne Dyer, who has been widely attributed with the quote, "Successful people make money. It's not that people who make money become successful, but that successful people attract money. They bring success to what they do."

Finally, another more financially-oriented definition of success is "The world defines success in terms of achieving one's goal, acquiring wealth, status, prestige and power."[2]

I will stop here and leave you to contemplate how you would answer the question of whether money and success are one and the same, before you turn the page.

Are Money and Success the Same Thing? – Part 2

I left you to contemplate some very insightful definitions and interpretations of success and how you would answer the question "Are money and success the same thing?" After re-reading those definitions and interpretations, my answer is that money and success are not one and the same.

That being said, I acknowledge that there is also a thread that closely connects success and money in many circumstances, such that the distinction is often blurred. Thus, I thought I would expand the question to include not only "Are money and success the same thing", but "Can money bring you success or success bring you money?" For those that feel I should be true to the original premise and question, I apologize for the re-phrasing, but hey, it's my book.

I believe there are circumstances where money can certainly help buy or leverage success, while in other situations, money may derail success. On the flip side, there appears to be circumstances where success brings you money.

So let's look at money and success in five of the key aspects of all our lives: family, career, health, spiritualism, and impact on society.

Family

When it comes to family, love and affection are familial success, not money. Nevertheless, we know families can be torn apart because of money; often because money is very tight, but also surprisingly often when there is too much money in the family.

With respect to family, money and success are clearly not the same thing. With respect to my re-phrased question, money will not bring you familial success, but in some circumstances, too much or too little money can tear away at the fabric of love and affection. Familial success in my opinion has little bearing on monetary success.

Career

If we are honest with ourselves, career success often leads to money and thus, this is the one aspect of our lives where I can see how a number of people equate money with success. Yes, there are many people for whom the job is the key and money is only secondary. But when we chat about someone, the first topic is usually about their job, which leads us wonder how much money they make. Or alternatively, "John makes so much money as a lawyer, he must be successful."

Thus, in the case of a career, even if you don't agree money and success are one in the same, I think you will agree there are career related circumstances where money can buy success or success can lead to money.

Health

Striving for money can affect one's health, be it striving for enormous wealth or enough to just support your family. Alternatively, money may relieve stress (no need to work hard) and buy you better health care.

In this circumstance, I think it is clear money and success are not the same thing. Having money won't mean you're successful in health (a.k.a. healthy, happy, active, or whatever other words you think define healthy), the only effect money can have on successful health is that it may enable you to buy the best healthcare possible. We all know the best healthcare does not guarantee successful health, but in very select cases, money may buy you health because of the access to care money provides.

In the end, Bob Marley said it best. On his deathbed he reportedly told his son Ziggy, "Money can't buy life".

Spirituality

This is one case where money is meaningless. People's spirituality comes from deep inside and money means nothing. However, it is somewhat ironic that when looking for money to build the addition to the church, synagogue or mosque, the first line of attack are those parishioners with money.

Impact on Society

Many people have a positive impact on society by giving their time for the greater good through volunteering. However, other people with money leverage their money to achieve real or perceived success through philanthropic deeds associated with money, such as building a hospital. Some people feel that is not true success, it is just a donation of money, while others would argue building a new hospital is a true success, regardless of whether the person just wrote a cheque or wrote a cheque and volunteered their time.

I think in this situation, money and success are not one and the same, but money can clearly have a positive impact on society and therefore, promote a form of success.

Conclusion

So, have we learned anything? I have learned (as I worked out this little philosophical debate in my head) that money and success are not one and the same, but do impact one another. Meaning in certain circumstances, money can influence success, and success can determine how much money you have.

On that note, I wish success to you all; however the heck you define it.

Intergenerational Communication Gap

In an article for CNBC, author Jessica Rao quotes Dr. Nancy Molitor, Clinical Psychologist and Public Education Coordinator for the American Psychological Association, as saying "Money is the most taboo, fearful subject that we can encounter as people."[3] An inability to discuss this taboo subject can have tremendous implications when taken in context of families and their money.

We are all familiar with the term "generation gap", but the lack of communication between generations can be very costly from both a financial and social perspective. The substantial wealth transfer taking place in Canada from parents to children, or from children to parents, makes clear communication between generations more important now than ever, yet the communication is mitigated by this taboo topic of money.

So what am I talking about? Let's consider Emily, a widower with two children. Emily's husband Bob passed away a couple years ago, but during his lifetime he amassed a significant estate due to the sale of his composite hockey stick company ten years ago. Emily has two children, John, a Bay Street lawyer making $800,000 a year and living in the upscale Toronto Rosedale neighborhood, and Susan, stuck in a bad marriage, who never finished university and married early.

Emily was brought up in an era where you didn't discuss your family assets with your children. John knows he will inherit millions of dollars when mom passes away, but gives it little thought as he is very comfortable and only acknowledges the inheritance in that he does not fully contribute to his Registered Retirement Savings Plan ("RRSP"). Susan on the other hand has had a somewhat strained relationship with her mom since her early marriage. Although they are currently on better terms, Susan is too proud to ask her mom for money and she does not think she would receive a warm reception even if she got over her pride and spoke to her mom about her finances. What Emily does not know is that Susan's husband is a cocaine user and she would like to leave him, but she is concerned about how she would survive. She would also give anything to go back to university to become a social worker, but that is currently just a dream.

Now imagine if everyone felt comfortable discussing money? Those that know Emily realize that she would give Susan some sort of early inheritance, but she does not want to insult Susan and she is not aware of her husband's issues and Susan's dreams. Further, imagine you were brought in as a family friend and could open up the intergenerational communication gap. Emily would be thrilled to provide an early inheritance to allow Susan to leave her husband and pay for the legal bills and, with Susan free of her husband, she would have the financial ability to go back to school to pursue her dream of being a social worker.

How is this gap bridged? I can't answer that question. But I know I have advised clients who have the financial means to try and have a heart-to-heart with their children in respect to their children's financial needs.

How about the alternative scenario of children who have the means to support less financially-secure parents? Sam is a widower. He was a factory worker who scrimped and saved to buy a house and put his two kids through school. Sam does not have enough money to retire and decides to obtain a reverse mortgage on his house such that when he dies, the mortgage owing is deducted from the sale proceeds of the house. This is often a costly form of financing. Sam is too proud to approach his children about his financial situation. However, if you were able to bridge the intergenerational gap, you would be able to inform Sam that his children, who are both successful, feel that they owe everything to Sam, and would be happy to either gift dad some money or provide him a loan at lower interest than the bank so he wouldn't have to reverse mortgage the house.

The two scenarios above have many variations. Pride, secrecy, and perceived "grabbing of the family money before the body is cold" prevent any kind of open communication.

I have no magical fix; however, if you are the parent, consider speaking to your children about their financial situations and dreams to see whether you can assist them in realizing those dreams. If you are tight for money in retirement, at minimum let your children know if you are undertaking a reverse mortgage or similar financial arrangement so they can potentially assist you or, at a minimum, understand that your estate has been compromised by a mortgage.

If you are the child in need, have a frank conversation with your parents to let them know your issues so they don't perceive you to be "money grabbing," or if you are a successful child with a parent of limited financial resources, offer to help or to pay for your financial advisor to sit down with them.

Are You Selfish with Your Money and Advice?

As discussed earlier in this chapter, many people do not like to talk about money, which in some cases is quite ludicrous, and potentially harmful in certain other situations.

But should this disinclination to discuss money extend to investment or cost-saving opportunities where you may be able to financially assist family, friends, and acquaintances? Are there situations in which you do not have to reveal personal financial details, such that one can disengage from the money taboo?

So, where am I going with this? Let me ask you the following questions:

1. If you are a stock picker and have a new favourite stock, would you inform your family, friends, and acquaintances about this stock?

2. What if you found a great cottage to rent this summer at a great price, but you could only use it for two weeks of the summer, would you inform your family or friends of its availability?

3. What if someone came to you with a private investment which you thought was the next Facebook, would you offer this opportunity to your family, friends, acquaintances, or clients?

4. What if you found a great real estate property you felt could be fixed up cheaply and flipped quickly, but you would be stretched to purchase it yourself. Would you offer a piece of this property to your family or friends?

5. Finally, what if you have a client or contact who is a distributor of Armani suits for men and Christian Louboutin shoes for women and they offer you a standard 50% discount and allow you to bring a guest, would you bring a guest?

Personally, I would answer yes to all the above and not think much about doing such. To me, if I can make money and also help someone make money or save money, I am happy to share the wealth, so to speak. In fact, I have done all of the above in some shape or form. This does not make me a good person (I have several other faults), but I am just not selfish where I can share the spoils of a good investment or opportunity.

However, some people are not as forthcoming. The question is why?

I see a couple of potential reasons.

The first and most justifiable reason is that although many people are willing to take a personal financial risk on a stock pick or investment opportunity, they do not want to be held responsible if others lose their money. I think this is a very valid concern. The only counter-argument I have for this concern is: if you know your family and friends well, you probably know to which people you can say "Here is the opportunity and here is the risk. You are a big boy or big girl, make your own decision, but I am partaking in this investment and if you follow suit, you do so with the same risk I have assumed."

I would suggest for the people in the subset above, most would probably inform family or friends about the cottage rental opportunity and the Armani suit or Christian Louboutin shoe sale, because in these cases, there is no risk of financial loss and blame, as you are just helping others save money.

For some people their actions maybe a result of their competitiveness in acquiring more than those around them, such that they feel more powerful with the exclusivity of being involved in these opportunities while excluding their family and friends.

These people feel that if their investments work out, they will have more money than their family, friends, and acquaintances and reinforce their financial superiority. In the case of the cottage they would not let others know about the deal they received, yet they would invite guests to the cottage to show it off. The same would go for the suits or shoes; they would rather show up in the Armani suit or Christian Louboutin shoes to reinforce their perceived power and status and would not want others to present the same image.

As I have stated on numerous occasions, I find the psychology of money intriguing. Think how you and the people you know would respond to the above five situations and whether these situations would provide a view into your/their financial psyches.

Investment Bravado, Little White Lies, and Why "Kiss and Tell" Investing Can Get You Shot

How many of us have heard cocktail bravado along these lines: "Boy did I make a killing buying gold" and "I bought my Mercedes with the profits I made on that tip"? Based upon these double-martini-induced boasts, Bill Gates and Warren Buffett should have multiple challengers for their positions as two of the world's wealthiest men. But like the Mercedes in your neighbour's driveway (that is in reality leased), and like that phantom profit from the stock tip, cocktail investment bravado is (more often than not, in my opinion), false or exaggerated.

Based upon 25 years of cocktail parties and my first-year university psychology course, it is my observation that people lie or exaggerate about their stock investments to maintain or enhance their self-esteem and their perceived social financial status. Robert Feldman, a University of Massachusetts psychologist says "People lie because they need to present themselves as competent and worthy. Money is one key way people feel they are valued."[4]

Exaggeration, tale-telling, even outright lying are merely tools to serve this ignoble enhancement of our own self-importance. Even on the macro level, we like sensationalized financial news. Ever wonder why the markets wander a few points up or down when the media throws around adjectives like "skyrocket" or "plummet"? Keeping the market interesting justifies our interest in it and, by extension, validates our collective social financial activity and identity. Not only do we need to lie to feel good about ourselves, we would rather hear sketchy hyperbole from borderline sources than bad news from an honest one.

In addition to the various types of investment bravado noted above, it is also my experience that investors are generally disinclined to admit their mistakes. Most investors seem to prefer smoke and mirrors and martinis to black coffee and straight talk. An unsettling dishonesty attaches itself to this disinclination to admit error, or respect those that do.

My persona on my blog is *The Blunt Bean Counter*. Believe it or not, some thought went into this moniker. I am blunt. I am also pretty open, much to my wife's chagrin. So if I think I am on to a good stock, I don't need to keep it to myself; if I get killed on a stock investment, I admit it. As it turns out, this "kiss and tell" philosophy on investing ended up being the conduit to a human psychology experiment in a national newspaper, so maybe in essence I am an amateur psychologist, even if not by intention.

You see, when Larry MacDonald asked if he could profile me for *The Globe and Mail*'s *Me and My Money* column[5], I knew I was going to do something somewhat controversial for it. *Me and My Money* is presented in a somewhat standard format of first discussing your investment philosophy, secondly informing the readers of some of your stock holdings, then thirdly informing the readers of your best and worst stock picks, and finally providing advice.

I knew from the outset that I was going to have the same stock as my worst and best pick, a first for the *Me and My Money* column as far as I know. That stock is Resverlogix ("RVX"), and if you have not read my tale detailing my ownership of this stock, read my blog post, *Resverlogix – A Cautionary Tale*.

I have no idea what the record is for comments on the *Me and My Money* column, but I am sure I am in the top ten. The comments started fast and furious.

Most centered on how I was greedy. I did not mind being called greedy, I was greedy with respect to the call options I held in RVX and I was cognizant of this greed and the risk I took because of this greed.

An example of some of the comments I received was: "Three animals in the market. The Bull. The Bear. The Pig. This is an example of being a pig."

However, after the initial avalanche of negative comments, suddenly there was a wave of support for the column starting with:

> "Thanks for this, we've all been there (at least those of us that are honest) but apparently some here are deluded enough to believe it can never happen to them."

> "Hey, it takes a lot of guts to come on a national website and admit to one's bone-headed investment moves... Great investors like Peter Lynch aren't born... They learned through trial and error."

These comments reflect the essence of what I am getting at. Few people are totally honest about their investing trials and tribulations, and even fewer admit them. I guess for many, money is a reflection of self-worth and success, and cocktail chatter allows them to espouse freely without address. For a selected few the bravado is warranted (although these people are typically not bragging in public); for some, they utilize selective disclosure (yes, they made a large profit on a certain stock or investment, they just have a slight memory lapse about the three other stocks they had significant losses on); and finally, for some, they are just trying to look good both to themselves and others, no matter if the tale is more fiction than fact.

As an observer of human investment behavior, I find it fascinating that many need to accentuate or exaggerate the positive, yet they are mute when their investments go sour.

Oh Those Sleepless Nights – What is Keeping You up at Night?

What is keeping you up at night? That is one loaded question. It may be a financial issue, a family issue, a business issue, or in my case, the sub sandwich with hot peppers I ate at 10 pm last night. All joking aside, this is a serious question and everyone from psychiatrists to financial consultants ask this question or a variation of it when meeting a new patient or client.

If you had asked me 25 or so years ago whether this question would have any relevance to me professionally other than from a financial perspective, I would have looked at you like you were crazy. However, as I look back over my career, I am amazed at how often I have been a psychologist to my clients and how often money issues are inter-twined or even secondary to family and personal issues. Analyzing sleep loss is a skillset I was not taught in university or in any of my Chartered Professional Accountant courses.

Despite my sometimes-amateur-psychologist status, it would be presumptuous of me to even consider providing advice of a psychological nature on non-financial matters. Thus, I will focus on the observations I have made over the course of my career in relation to financial matters that have kept my clients up at night.

As I reflect on this issue, I have come up with four primary observations:

Get Objective Advice

It is extremely difficult to solve complex problems by yourself. It is vitally important when you have significant financial issues keeping you up at night that you speak to someone who can provide objective financial advice (your accountant, financial planner, investment advisor, or a close friend). When one experiences a significant financial issue, it has been my experience that he/she loses perspective and fails to see the forest for the trees. Speaking to someone you trust implicitly who knows both your financial situation and your personality provides you with a detached, non-emotional perspective on your financial issues.

It Takes Time

Most financial problems are not immediately solvable. From excessive debt, to funding your child's education, to fluctuations in foreign currency causing the cost of goods in your business to rise dramatically, the sad truth is that time is often the only answer and the sooner that fact is accepted, the better. Whether it is the slow process of putting an actionable debt reduction budget in place, the many years it takes to fund a Registered Education Savings Plan ("RESP"), or cutting back on costs to offset foreign currency fluctuations and/or wait out a reversal in those rates, in each case, time is the only answer.

Some Financial Problems Don't Have a Solution

Thankfully these instances have been few and far between, but the saddest moments in my career have been those where a financial problem was not solvable. The typical situation where this occurs is when a once-successful business is careening towards bankruptcy because of technological changes, competitors outsourcing to a low-cost country, or just plain business mismanagement. These situations are very complex. Often the person is a long-time client whom I have gotten to know on a personal basis and I have to tell them they need to close their business (this would be last resort advice after all other alternatives have been exhausted).

This advice often leads to confrontation because (a) the client's self-worth and net-worth often revolve around their business; and (b) the client's own solution is typically to throw more money at the problem while I am trying to prevent throwing good money after bad to ensure they still have resources once the business is closed.

In the end, all a financial advisor can hope for is that the client eventually realizes their situation is not fixable, and begrudgingly takes your advice and conserves their remaining resources.

The Moment of Absolute Certainty Never Arises

One of my favourite quotes is from S.H. Payer's poem *Live Each Day to the Fullest.*[6] In his poem he states, "The moment of absolute certainty never arrives". Whether a decision is financial or personal, it has been my experience that often people are frozen in their tracks with indecision and cannot take action on their issue until they feel they have found that moment of certainty. However, we all know that moment very rarely identifies itself (or if it does, often it is not in a timely manner). That is why I love this quote. Time constraints often force us to deal with an issue before there is certainty, and those people who make the best decision under the circumstances and move forward without regret or second-guessing themselves are best equipped to solve and deal with their issues, even if the decision does not turn out to be correct.

Although the above discussion is not technically related to tax, business, or investment advice, sometimes general life advice is worth far more than income tax or financial advice and is definitely cheaper.

---

1 Wooden, John, and Steve Jamison. *Wooden on Leadership.* New York: McGraw-Hill, 2005. 8.

2 Hata, Paul. "Success According To The Bible." Findinarticles.com. July 31, 2008.

3 Rao, Jessica. "All In The Family—Making Money Talk Easier." CNBC. February 8, 2010.

4 Medintz, Scott. "Secrets, Lies and Money." *Money*, April 1, 2005.

5 MacDonald, Larry. "Me and My Money: Investor Does His Homework on Individual Stocks." The Globe and Mail. February 11, 2011.

6 Payer, S. H. *Live Each Day to The Fullest.* American Greetings, 1980.

Chapter 5

Audits and Being Audited – Minimizing the Damage

CRA Audit – Will I Be Selected?

I am often asked how the Canada Revenue Agency ("CRA") selects tax payers for audit. Through experience I know certain taxpayers, certain claims, and certain industries seem to trigger audits. With that in mind, I will list below what I have seen and how I believe the CRA selects certain individuals and businesses for audit.

Reasons for Individuals and Corporations

I would suggest there is nothing worse than a scorned lover, a business partner you have had a falling out with, or a dismissed employee to trigger a CRA audit. These individuals know your little secrets: a cash deal here, an offshore account there, and a conference you expensed that was really a vacation. These people are also vindictive, and in some cases they make statements and claims that are not factual in nature; however, the claims are enough to bring the CRA to your door.

CRA also loves net worth audits. These are audits undertaken because you live in a 3,000 square foot home, have a Porsche and kids in private school, and yet show minimal income on your tax return. Typically the CRA either stumbles upon these situations, or information from one of the individuals noted in the preceding paragraph provides a lead.

Reasons Specific to Individuals

We see far more desk audits (information requests in regard to certain deductions claimed) than full blown audits for individuals. You can expect an inquiry if you claim any of the following:

- a significant interest expense
- an allowable business investment loss (usually if you held shares in a bankrupt private Canadian company)

- tuition from a university outside Canada (typically the child and parent are tied together as most children transfer $5,000 of their tuition claim to their parents)

- a child care claim for a nanny even if you have filed a T4 for the nanny with the CRA

In all the above cases you are just providing back-up information, these are not audits.

In past years individuals who purchased any tax shelter other than an oil and gas or mineral flow-through have been audited. However, in most cases the CRA is auditing the tax shelter itself and the individual investors just get reassessed personally.

Full-blown audits seem to occur with regularity in regard to individuals who earn commission income or self-employment income and claim expenses against that income. In those cases, the CRA gravitates to auto expense claims, requesting log books they know one in 100 people actually keep, and advertising and promotion expenses they consider personal in nature.

Reasons Specific to Corporations

Corporations seem to be selected for three distinct reasons.

They carry on a business that is the CRA's flavour of the year; some prior flavours have been pharmacies, contractors and the real estate industry, and any other industry the CRA feels is a "cash is king" industry.

Corporations file a General Index of Financial Information ("GIFI"). This information provides a comparative year-to-year summary of income and expenses. It is suspected by many accountants that the

CRA uses this information to review year-to-year expense and income variances of the filing corporation and to also compare corporations within a similar industry sector to identify those outside the standard ratios, but we don't know that for certain.

The final reason is that it is just your turn. I have no knowledge of this, but it seems like the CRA just runs down a list and if you don't get caught with regard to reason one or two, your turn just eventually comes up.

In all cases it is imperative you keep your source documents to provide to the auditor. It is also vitally important if you (and not your accountant) are meeting with the auditor that you try and keep your cool. In the end, the auditor is just doing his or her job, and if you treat them badly you are not doing yourself any favours.

Dealing with the Canada Revenue Agency

There are six typical circumstances by which an individual may end up dealing with the CRA.

The least worrisome of the six situations is where you initiate contact with the CRA to report a late income tax slip (such as a T3 or T5 slip), or you realize you missed a deduction or credit (such as a donation slip, medical expense or Registered Retirement Savings Plan "RRSP" receipt). These situations are very straightforward and relatively painless. You or your accountant file a "T1 Adjustment Request" using form *T1-ADJ E* to report the additional income or claim the additional expense or credit. You would typically attach the receipt to the form and most of these requests are processed without further query from the CRA.

The second circumstance is where you receive an information request from the CRA. These requests often strike fear into my clients' hearts, but are typically harmless. In this situation, the CRA usually sends a letter asking for back-up relating to a deduction or credit claimed on the return. Generally these requests by the CRA are to provide support for items such as a donation tax credit, a medical expense claim, a child care expense claim, a children's fitness tax credit claim or an interest expense claim. These requests are fairly common and, more often than not, relate to personal income tax returns that are e-filed. You have 30 days to respond to these requests; however, time extensions are typically granted if you call the CRA and request it.

The third situation, and a step up on the anxiety meter, is the receipt of a Notice of Reassessment ("NOR") from the CRA. An NOR may be issued for numerous reasons, such as not responding to an information request, the receipt by the CRA of a T3/T4/T5 slip that was not reported in your tax return, or a reassessment based on an audit or review of your tax return as discussed below.

The fourth circumstance is typically not pleasant. In this scenario, the CRA has selected you for an audit, either randomly or because you have come to their attention for some reason. An audit can take the form of a desk audit, which is less intrusive, or a full-blown field audit. Desk audits are typically undertaken to review a specific item that the CRA finds unusual in nature, and you have 30 days to respond.

A full-blown audit could encompass a review of self-employment expenses, significant expense or deduction claims, or a full review of your personal or corporate income tax filings for a specific year or multiple years. In this situation, you will be sent a letter requesting certain information and you will be required to provide such to a CRA auditor. This process could take months, and if the CRA auditor is not satisfied by your documentation or reasons for claiming certain expenses or deductions, they will issue a revised NOR.

Upon receipt of the reassessment, you will have to determine, likely in conjunction with your accountant, whether the CRA's assessment is justified. If you don't feel it is justified, you need to consider if the amount of reassessed tax is significant enough to warrant the time and energy to "fight" the reassessment. If you decide to fight the reassessment, you and/or your accountant would file a "Notice of Objection" using form T400A. In this fifth situation, the Notice of Objection would state the facts of your situation and the reasons that you object to the CRA's reassessment. The objection will then be reviewed (probably months later) by a CRA representative, and you can make and support your case as to why the CRA has incorrectly assessed or reassessed you.

It is very important to make sure that you file a Notice of Objection on a timely basis. For an individual (other than a trust), the time limit for filing an objection is the later of these two dates: one year after the date of the returns filing deadline, or 90 days after the day the CRA mailed the reassessment. For corporations, the time limit is 90 days.

Finally, the sixth and final situation (and last resort) is to go to tax court because your Notice of Objection was not successful. There is an informal tax court procedure if your income tax owing is less than $25,000. Where the income tax owing exceeds $25,000, the process becomes formal and is costly and time-consuming.

The above summarizes the various circumstances and situations in which you may deal with the CRA in any given year. Hopefully if you have any contact with the CRA, it is only in connection to situation one or two.

How Long Do I Have to Keep My Income Tax Records?

A common question I receive from my clients is "How long do I have to keep my income tax records?" For anyone actually interested, the CRA created guide *RC4409*, called "Keeping Records"[1], which details everything you want to know about your record keeping and more. This guide is most applicable to individuals that carry on a business, and to corporations.

Now I know you are waiting with bated breath for the answer, but you will have to humour me while I provide some background detail.

Firstly, the CRA recognizes records were traditionally kept in paper format, and that today many kinds of electronic records are kept by computer systems. The CRA says electronic records may be stored on a computer, network, CD, DVD, tape, or cartridge.

Notwithstanding the format of the records, supporting documents are required. The supporting documents can be kept in any of the above formats.

Finally, you are required to keep your source documents, which include sales invoices, purchase receipts, contracts, bank deposit slips, and cancelled cheques. They also include cash register receipts, credit card receipts, and purchase orders to name a few.

Okay, now that I have kept you in suspense, here is the answer. The CRA says "As a general rule, you must keep all of the records and supporting documents that are required to determine your tax obligations and entitlements for a period of **six years from the end of the last tax year to which they relate**. The six-year retention period under the *Income Tax Act* begins at the end of the tax year to which the records relate."[2] *Thus, in many cases you are actually keeping your records seven years.*

The fact that you must retain your records for at least six years does not mean you will be audited for six years at a time. Typically you are barred from being reassessed by the CRA three years from the mailing date of your Notice of Assessment ("NOA"), assuming there is no tax evasion and loss years are not still open.

A word of caution, ensure you keep your source documents; they are key to satisfying many an auditor. In addition, documents that substantiate the cost base of real estate, shares, etc, should be kept longer than six years.

Where you are an individual and do not carry on a business, the CRA says on their website that you are still subject to the six-year retention period. They have also said the following with respect to electronic tax return filings:

> Canadians who plan to file their income tax and benefit returns electronically, or who do not file information slips and receipts with their paper-filed return, should keep their tax records on hand in case they are contacted by the Canada Revenue Agency (CRA).

> After returns are filed, the CRA begins work to verify the income reported, as well as the credits and deductions claimed. These reviews are an important way that the CRA makes sure that Canadians are paying their taxes. ...

> ... Some of the first reviews of deductions and credits are done when returns are filed, and before taxpayers receive

their notice of assessment. However, most reviews take place later in the year, as the CRA works to verify the information on an individual's return and compare it with the information provided by other parties, such as an employer, a spouse, or a common-law partner.

During this review process, the CRA may contact taxpayers to ask for more information on income sources or dependants, and may ask for copies of receipts or information slips to support claims, related to:

- medical expenses

- charitable donations

- child care expenses

- spouse or child support payments

- moving expenses

Keeping your records on hand makes it easier to respond to these requests, and will help you explain your tax and benefit situation to the CRA if you do not agree with your reassessment.

Receiving a request for receipts or documentation does not mean you are being audited by the CRA. When an individual is selected for an audit, the CRA tells them that their tax and benefit situation is being reviewed and calls to arrange a meeting to begin the audit.[3]

The CRA's Matching Program – Mismatch and You May Be Assessed a 20% Penalty

How can you be issued a 20% penalty for missing information the CRA has on hand? Read on and you will find out!

Each fall, the CRA's matching program issues Notice of Reassessments to Canadians whose reported income on their income tax return did not match the CRA's records. Some of these income tax filers will be assessed penalties of 20% on income not reported. Yes, that is *income not reported, not tax underpaid!* This penalty applies to income tax information your employer or financial institution provided to the CRA which was not reported on your return. In most cases, the omission of income was purely unintentional.

What is wrong with this picture? How can one be considered to not have reported income that the CRA has in its database? Is this not a penalty for failing to confirm income, as opposed to not reporting income?

The Matching Program

The CRA's matching program catches the non-reporting of income every fall. Each year the CRA checks the T-slip information in its database against Canadian taxpayers' income tax returns to ensure the reported T-slip income matches. Where the income filed by a tax-payer does not match the CRA's database records, an income tax reassessment is mailed to the taxpayer asking for the income tax due. If the taxpayer is a first time offender, they are just assessed the actual income tax owing and possibly some interest. If this is the second occurrence in the last four years, a 20% penalty of the unreported income is assessed.

The Penalty Provision

Under subsection 163(1) of the *Income Tax Act*, where a taxpayer has failed to report income twice within a four-year period, he/she will be subject to a penalty. The penalty is calculated as 10% of the amount you failed to report the second time. A corresponding provincial penalty is also applied, so the total penalty is 20% of the unreported income.[4]

Ouch! Is This Fair?

I find this penalty unfair for the following reasons:

1. It is excessive. I can accept a penalty of 5%, maybe 10%, but 20%?

2. The penalty can be levied even if you owe no income tax, e.g. if someone in Ontario fails to report a T4 slip with $5,000 of employment income and the slip also reported $2,325 of income tax deducted, they would owe no income tax, as the maximum marginal income tax rate of 46.41% was applied (ignoring Ontario supertax). However, if you had failed to report income in any of the three prior years, the penalty under subsection 163(1) would be $1,000 (20% of $5,000), even though you owed no income tax and the CRA was provided this information by your employer.

3. The penalty can vary wildly on the exact same total of non-reported income. If you fail to report $2,000 two years ago and fail to report $100 this year, your penalty is $20. However, if you failed to report $100 two years ago and failed to report $2,000 this year, the penalty is $400! That is a huge difference in penalties for the exact same total of unreported income.

4. Most penalties relate to T-slips taxpayers did not knowingly ignore or evade. In most cases, the missing income relates

to T-slips lost in the mail or sent to the wrong address. Also, many T-slips are now issued online and easy to miss.

According to an article by Tom McFeat of CBC News, the number of Canadians penalized for this repeated failure to report income totalled over 81,000 in 2011, with an income tax cost of slightly over $78,000,000.[5]

To be clear, my issue with this penalty is that taxpayers in most cases are being penalized where there is no intent to hide income and the CRA receives that information. However, I am not as forgiving with the non-reporting of rental income, capital gains, or self-employment, which relies on taxpayer honesty.

Tax Tip for T-slips Received After You Filed Your Tax Return

I think most people will agree that this penalty is excessive, so here is a quick tip. If you received a T-slip after filing your tax return and ignored the slip since it was a small amount, dig it out tonight and file a T1 Adjustment Request as soon as possible before the matching program gets you. Even a small $10 missed slip will start your clock ticking for a potentially larger penalty if you miss reporting income again in the subsequent three years.

[Author's Note: The 2015 Federal budget proposes to address the above noted deficiency by tying the penalty to the income tax owing as a result of any non-reporting.]

---

1 "RC4409 Keeping Records." Canada Revenue Agency. Revised 2011.

2 Ibid., 7.

3 Canada Revenue Agency Press Release. "Keep Your Records to Support Your Income Tax and Benefit Return." Canada Revenue Agency. April 8, 2009.

4 *Income Tax Act*, RSC 1985, c 1 (5th Supp), s 163(1).

5 McFeat, Tom. "Tough Tax Penalty Raises Fairness Concerns." CBC News. April 19, 2012.

Chapter 6

Tax Topics - All You Ever Wanted to Know but Were Afraid to Ask

Tax-Loss Selling – 2014

I am writing about tax-loss selling because every year around the holidays, people get busy with their holiday shopping and forget to sell the "dogs" in their portfolio, and as a consequence, they pay unnecessary income tax on their capital gains in April. Additionally, while most investment advisors are pretty good at contacting their clients to discuss possible tax-loss selling, I am still amazed each year at how many advisors do not discuss the issue with their clients. So if you have an advisor, ensure you are in contact to discuss your realized capital gain/loss situation and other planning options (if you have to initiate the contact, consider that a huge black mark against your advisor).

I would suggest that the best stock trading decisions are often not made while waiting in line to pay for your child's Christmas gift. Yet, many people persist in waiting until the third week of December to trigger their capital losses to use against their current or prior years' capital gains. To avoid this predicament, you may wish to set aside some time to review your 2014 capital gain/loss situation in a calm, methodical manner. You can then execute your trades on a timely basis knowing you have considered all the variables associated with your tax gain/loss selling.

I would like to provide one caution in respect of tax-loss selling. You should be very careful if you plan to repurchase the stocks you sell (see superficial loss discussion below). The reason for this is that you are subject to market vagaries for 30 days. I have seen people sell stocks for tax-loss purposes, with the intention of re-purchasing those stocks and one or two of the stocks take off during the 30 day wait period and the cost to repurchase is far in excess of their tax savings. Thus, you should first and foremost consider selling your "dog stocks" that you and/or your advisor no longer wish to own. If you then need to crystallize additional losses, be wary if you are planning to sell and buy back the same stock.

Below, I will take you through each step of the tax-loss selling process. In addition, I will provide a planning technique to create a capital gain where you have excess capital losses, and a technique to create a capital loss where you have taxable gains.

Reporting Capital Gains and Capital Losses – the Basics

All capital gain and capital loss transactions for 2014 will have to be reported on Schedule 3 of your 2014 personal income tax return. You then subtract the total capital gains from the total capital losses and multiply the net capital gain/loss by ½. That amount becomes your taxable capital gain or net capital loss for the year. If you have a taxable capital gain, the amount is carried forward to the tax return jacket on line 127. For example, if you have a capital gain of $120 and a capital loss of $30 in the year, ½ of the net amount of $90 would be taxable and $45 would be carried forward to line 127. The taxable capital gains are then subject to income tax at your marginal income tax rate.

Capital Losses

If you have a net capital loss in the current year, the loss cannot be deducted against other sources of income. However, the net capital loss may be carried back to offset any taxable capital gains incurred in any of the three preceding years, or, if you did not have any gains in the three prior years, the net capital loss becomes an amount that can be carried forward indefinitely to utilize against any future taxable capital gains.

Planning Preparation

I suggest you start your preliminary planning immediately. These are the steps I recommend you take:

1. Retrieve your 2013 Notice of Assessment ("NOA"). In the verbiage discussing changes and other information, if you have a capital loss carryforward, the balance will be reported. This information may also be accessed online if you have registered with the Canada Revenue Agency ("CRA").

2. If you do not have capital losses to carry forward, retrieve your 2011, 2012 and 2013 income tax returns to determine if you have taxable capital gains upon which you can carry back a current year capital loss. On an Excel spreadsheet or multi-column paper, note any taxable capital gains you reported in 2011, 2012 and 2013.

3. For each of 2011, 2012 and 2013, review your income tax returns to determine if you applied a net capital loss from a prior year on line 253 of your income tax return. If yes, reduce the taxable capital gain on your excel spreadsheet by the loss applied.

4. Finally, if you had net capital losses in 2012 or 2013, review whether you carried back those losses to 2011 or 2012 on form T1A "Request for Loss Carryback" of your income tax return. If you carried back a loss to either 2011 or 2012, reduce the gain on your spreadsheet by the loss carried back.

5. If after adjusting your taxable gains by the net capital losses under steps 3 and 4, you still have a positive balance remaining for any of the years 2011, 2012 and 2013, you can potentially generate an income tax refund by carrying back a net capital loss from 2014 to any or all of 2011, 2012 and 2013.

6. If you have an investment advisor, call and request a realized capital gain/loss summary from January 1st to date to determine if you are in a net gain or loss position. If you trade yourself, ensure you update your capital gain/loss schedule (or Excel spreadsheet, whatever you use) for the year.

Now that you have all the information you need, it is time to be strategic about how to use your losses.

Basic Use of Losses

For discussion purposes, let's assume the following:

- 2014: realized capital loss of $30,000

- 2013: taxable capital gain of $15,000

- 2012: taxable capital gain of $5,000

- 2011: taxable capital gain of $7,000

Based on the above, you will be able to carry back your $15,000 net capital loss ($30,000 x ½) from 2014 against the $7,000 and $5,000 taxable capital gains in 2011 and 2012, respectively, and apply the remaining $3,000 against your 2013 taxable capital gain. As you will not have absorbed $12,000 ($15,000 of original gain less the $3,000 net capital loss carryback) of your 2013 taxable capital gains, you may want to consider whether you want to sell any "dogs" in your port-folio so that you can carry back the additional 2014 net capital loss to offset the remaining $12,000 taxable capital gain realized in 2013. Alternatively, if you have capital gains in 2014, you may want to sell stocks with unrealized losses to fully or partially offset those capital gains.

Creating Gains When You Have Unutilized Losses

Where you have a large capital loss carryforward from prior years and it is unlikely that the losses will be utilized either due to the quantum of the loss, or because you are out of the stock market and don't anticipate any future capital gains of any kind (such as the sale of real estate), it may make sense for you to purchase a flow-through limited partnership ("FTLP") (be aware; although there are income tax benefits to purchasing an FTLP, there are also investment risks).

Purchasing an FTLP will provide you with a write-off against regular income pretty much equal to the cost of the unit, and any future capital gain can be reduced or eliminated by your capital loss carryforward. For example, if you have a net capital loss carryforward of $75,000 and you purchase a flow-through investment in 2014 for $20,000, you would get approximately $20,000 in cumulative tax deductions in 2014 and 2015, the majority typically coming in the year of purchase. Depending upon your marginal income tax rate, the deductions could save you upwards of $9,200 in taxes. When you sell the unit, a capital gain will arise. This is because the $20,000 income tax deduction reduces your adjusted cost base ("ACB") from $20,000 to nil (there may be other adjustments to the cost base). Assuming you sell the unit in 2016 and you have a capital gain of say $18,000, the entire $18,000 gain will be eliminated by your capital loss carryforward. Thus, in this example, you would have total after-tax proceeds of $27,200 ($18,000 +$9,200 in tax savings) on a $20,000 investment.

Donation of Flow-through Shares

Prior to March 22, 2011, you could donate your publicly listed flow-through shares ("FTS") to charity and obtain a donation receipt for the fair market value ("FMV") of the shares. In addition, the capital gain you incurred (FMV less your ACB [ACB is typically nil or very low after claiming flow-through deductions]) would be exempted from income tax. However, for any flow-through agreement entered into after March 21, 2011, the tax benefit relating to the capital gain is eliminated or reduced. Simply put (the rules are more complicated, especially for limited partnership units converted to mutual funds, and an advisor should be consulted), if you paid $25,000 for your FTS, only the gain in excess of $25,000 will now be exempt and the first $25,000 will be taxable.

So if you are donating FTS to charity this year, ensure you speak to your accountant as the rules can be complex and you may create an unwanted capital gain.

Superficial Losses

One must always be cognizant of the superficial loss rules. Essentially, if you or your spouse (either directly or through an Registered Retirement Savings Plan ["RRSP"]) purchase an identical share 30 calendar days before or after a sale of shares, the capital loss is denied and added to the cost base of the new shares acquired.

Disappearing Dividend Income

Every year, I ask at least one or two clients why their dividend income is lower on their personal income tax return. Typically the answer is, "Oops, it is lower because I sold a stock early in the year that I forgot to tell you about." Thus, if you manage you own investments, you may wish to review your dividend income being paid each month or quarter with that of last year's to see if it is lower. If the dividend income is lower because you have sold a stock, confirm you have picked up that capital gain in your calculations.

Creating Capital Losses – Transferring Losses to a Spouse Who Has Gains

In certain cases you can use the superficial loss rules to your benefit. If you plan early enough, you can essentially use the superficial rules to transfer a capital loss you cannot use to your spouse. A quick recap: if you sell shares to realize a capital loss and then have your spouse repurchase the same shares within 30 days, your capital loss will be denied as a superficial loss and added to the ACB of the shares repurchased by your spouse. Your spouse then must hold the shares for more than 30 days, and once 30 days pass; your spouse can then sell the shares to realize a capital loss that can be used to offset their realized capital gains. Alternatively, you may be able to just sell shares to your spouse and elect out of certain provisions in the *Income Tax Act*.

Both these scenarios are complicated and subject to missteps, thus you should not undertake these transactions without first obtaining professional advice.

Settlement Date

It is my understanding that the settlement date for stocks in 2014 will be Wednesday, December 24. Thus, you must sell any stock you want to crystallize the gain or loss in 2014 by December 24, 2014.

Summary

As discussed above, there are a multitude of factors to consider when tax-loss selling. It would therefore be prudent to start planning early, so that you can consider all your options rather than frantically selling via your mobile device while sitting on Santa's lap in the third week of December.

Personal-Use Property – Taxable Even If the Picasso Walks out the Door

What do stamps, duck decoys, hockey cards, dolls, coins, comics, art, books, toys, and lamps have in common?

If you answered that the collection of these items are hobbies, you are partially correct. What you may not know is that these hobbies also generate some of the most valuable collectibles in the world.

The taxation of personal-use property is complicated, especially when a collector dies and leaves these types of collectibles to the next generation. The collectibles can cause rifts amongst family members. The rifts may occur in regard to which child is entitled to ownership of which collectible and whether the income tax liability related to these collectibles should be reported by the family members.

Let's examine these issues one at a time. Many of these collectibles somehow miss being included in wills. I think the reason for this is twofold. The first reason is that some parents truly do not recognize the value of some of these collectibles, and the second (more likely) reason is that they do realize the value and they don't want these assets to come to the attention of the tax authorities by including them in their will (a third potential reason is that your parents frequented discos in the 70s, and they took Gloria Gaynor singing "walk out the door" literally – but I digress and I am showing my age).

Two issues arise when collectibles are ignored in wills:

1. The parents take a huge leap of faith that their children will sort out the ownership of these assets in a detached and non-emotional manner, which is very unlikely, especially if the collectibles have wide-ranging values.

2. The collectibles (in many cases) will trigger an income tax liability if the deceased was the last surviving spouse, or the collectibles were not left to a surviving spouse.

Collectibles are considered personal-use property. Personal-use property is divided into two subcategories: one being listed personal property ("LPP"), the category most of the above collectibles fall into; and the other category being regular personal-use property ("PUP").

PUP "refers to items that are owned primarily for the personal use or enjoyment of your family and yourself. It includes all personal and household items such as furniture, automobiles, boats, a cottage, and other similar properties."[1] These types of property, other than the cottage or certain types of antiques and collectibles (e.g. classic automobiles), typically decline in value. You cannot claim a capital loss on PUP.

For PUP, where the proceeds received when you sell the item are less than $1,000 (or if the market value of the item is less than $1,000 when your parent passes away), there is no capital gain or loss. Where the proceeds of disposition are greater than $1,000 (or the market value at the date a parent passes away is greater than $1,000), there may be a capital gain. Where the proceeds are greater than $1,000 (or the market value is greater than $1,000 when a parent passes away), the ACB will be deemed to be the greater of either $1,000 or the actual ACB (i.e. generally the amount originally paid) in determining any capital gain that must be reported. Thus, the CRA essentially provides you with a minimum ACB of $1,000.

LPP typically increases in value over time. LPP includes all or part of any interest in or any right to the following properties:[2]

- prints, etchings, drawings, paintings, sculptures, or other similar works of art

- jewellery

- rare folios, rare manuscripts, or rare books

- stamps

- coins

Capital gains on LPP are calculated in the same manner as capital gains on PUP. Capital losses on LPP where the ACB exceeds the $1,000 minimum may be applied against future LPP capital gains, although as noted above, these types of items tend to increase in value.

The taxation of collectibles becomes especially interesting upon the death of the last spouse to die. There is a deemed disposition of the asset at death. For example, if your parents were lucky or smart enough to have purchased art from a member of the Group of Seven many years ago for say $2,000 and the art is now worth $50,000, there would be a capital gain of $48,000 upon the death of the last spouse (assuming the art had been transferred to that spouse upon the death of the first spouse). That deemed capital gain has to be reported on the terminal income tax return of the last surviving spouse. The income tax on that gain could be as high as $11,000.

The above-noted tax liability is why some families decide to let the collectibles "walk out the door". However, by allowing the collectibles to walk, family members who are executors can potentially be held liable for any income tax not reported by the estate, and thus should tread carefully in distributing assets such as collectibles.

If you are an avid collector, it may make sense to have the collectibles initially purchased in a child's name. You should speak to a tax professional before considering such, as you need to be careful in navigating the income attribution tax rules.

Where the above alternative is not practical or desirable, you should ensure that you have set aside funds or even taken out life insurance in order to cover the income tax liability stemming from these collectibles that may arise upon your death.

The Income Tax Implications of Purchasing a Rental Property

Many people have been burned by the stock market over the past decade, and find it to be a confusing and complex place. As a consequence, some people have far more comfort owning real estate (in particular, rental real estate). While both stocks and real estate have their own risks, some proportion of both these types of assets should typically be owned in a properly allocated investment portfolio.

The determination of a property's location and the issue as to what is a fair price to pay for any rental property is a book unto its own. For purposes of this discussion, let's assume you have resolved these two issues and are about to purchase a rental property. The following are some of the income tax and business issues you need to consider when purchasing a rental property:

Legal Structure

Your first decision when purchasing a rental property is whether to incorporate a company to acquire the property, or to purchase the property in a personal/partnership capacity of some kind. If you are purchasing a one-off property, in most cases (as long as you can cover any potential legal liability with insurance), there is minimal benefit of using a corporate structure.

In most provinces there is no tax benefit to purchasing a property in a corporation due to the fact that the corporate income tax rate for passive rental income is approximately 46%. Given there is no income tax incentive to utilize a corporation, when you include the cost of the professional fees associated with a corporation, in most cases, the use of a corporation does not make sense (unless you do so for creditor-proofing reasons).

In addition, if the property is purchased in one's personal capacity, any operating losses can be used to offset other personal income. If the property runs an operating loss and is owned by a corporation, those losses will remain in the corporation and can only be utilized once the rental property incurs a profit.

If you decide to purchase a rental property in your personal capacity, you must then decide whether the legal structure will be sole ownership, a partnership, or a joint venture. Many people purchase rental properties with friends or relatives, and/or want to have the property held jointly with a spouse. Where it has been determined that the property will be owned with another person, most people fail to give any consideration to signing a partnership or joint venture agreement in regards to the property. This can be a costly oversight if the relationship between the property owners goes astray or there is disagreement between the parties in terms of how the rental property should be run.

One should also note that there are subtle differences between a partnership and a joint venture. This is a complicated legal issue, but for income tax purposes if the property is a partnership, the capital cost allowance ("CCA"), known to many as depreciation, must be claimed at the partnership level. Thus, the partners share in the CCA claim. However, if the property is purchased as a joint venture, each venturer can claim their own CCA, regardless of what the other person has done. This is a subtle, but significant difference.

Allocation of Purchase Price

Once the rental property is purchased, you must allocate the purchase price between land and building. Land is not depreciable for income tax purposes, so you will typically want to allocate the greatest proportion of the purchase price to the building which can be depreciated at 4%, assuming a residential rental property (commercial properties can be depreciated at 6% in certain circumstances) on a declining basis per year. Most people do not have any hard data to support the allocation (the amount insured or realty tax bill may be useful), so it has become somewhat standard to allocate the purchase price as 75%-80% to the building, and 20%-25% to the land. However, where you have some support for another allocation, you should consider use of that allocation. Typically for condominium purchases, no allocation (or, at maximum, an allocation of 10%) is assigned to land.

Repairs and Maintenance

If you are purchasing a property and it is not in a condition to rent immediately, typically those expenses must be capitalized to the cost of the building and depreciation will only commence once the building is available for use. When a building is purchased and is immediately available for rent, or has been owned for some time and then requires some work to be done, you must review all significant repairs to determine if they can be considered a betterment to the property or if the repairs simply return the property back to its original state. If a repair betters the property, the CRA's position set forth in Interpretation Bulletin 128R, paragraph 4, is that the repair should be capitalized and not expensed.[3] This is often a bone of contention between taxpayers and the CRA.

CCA

CCA (i.e. depreciation for tax purposes) is a double-edged sword. Where a property generates net income, depreciation can be claimed to the extent of the property's net income. Generally, you cannot create a rental loss with tax depreciation unless the rental/leasing property is a principal business corporation. The depreciation claim tends to create positive cash flow once the property is fully rented, as the depreciation either eliminates or, at minimum, reduces the income tax owing in any year (depreciation is a non-cash deduction, thereby saving actual cash with no outlay of cash). Many people use the cash-flow savings that result from the depreciation claim to aggressively pay down the mortgage on the rental property. The downside to claiming tax depreciation over the years is that upon the sale of the property, all the tax depreciation claimed in prior years is added back into income in the year of sale (assuming the property is sold for an amount greater than the original cost of the rental property). This add-back of prior years' tax depreciation is known as recapture.

People who have owned a rental property for a long period sometimes reach a point in time where they have such large recapture tax to pay; they don't want to sell the rental property. Personally, I do not agree with this position, since it is really a question of what your net position will be upon a sale and if you are selling the property at a good price. However, recapture is always an issue to be considered, especially for older properties that have been depreciating for years.

Reasonable Expectation of Profit Test

Previously, if a rental property historically incurred losses for a period of time, the CRA may have challenged the deductibility of these losses on the basis that the taxpayer had no "reasonable expectation of profit". Fortunately, the CRA's powers with respect to the enforcement of this test have been severely limited. The test has been reviewed by the Supreme Court of Canada, and their view is that where the activity lacks any element of personal benefit and where the activity is not a hobby (i.e. it has been organized and carried on as a legitimate commercial activity), "the test should be applied sparingly and with a latitude favouring the taxpayer, whose business judgement may have been less than competent."[4] Consequently, concerns previously held with respect to utilizing losses from rental properties, even if the properties were not profitable for some period of time, are now mitigated.

Purchasing a rental property requires a considerable amount of thought and due diligence prior to the actual acquisition. Having a basic understanding of the income tax consequences can assist in making the final determination to purchase the rental property.

The Income-Tax-Planning Tail Wagging the Tax Dodge

It has been my experience that many people are so averse to paying income taxes that they dive into very shortsighted income tax plans oblivious to the consequences. I believe in minimizing income taxes to the greatest extent possible, however you cannot tax plan in isolation.

Let's get to some examples.

In many Canadian families, the high-income earner either contributes to their own RRSP or makes a spousal contribution; in both cases the higher-income-earning spouse receives the income tax deduction at their marginal income tax rate. However, over the years I have seen many people so focused on the potential income tax savings an RRSP contribution will garner, that they also make RRSP contributions for their stay-at-home spouse, to utilize their spouse's RRSP contribution room (these are not spousal contributions). But, because the spouse has minimal or no income, no income tax refund is generated and the RRSP deduction is not utilized (it can, however, be carried forward to a future year).

The ultimate example of the "tax tail wagging the tax dodge" is the purchase of a flow-through limited partnership unit ("FTLP"). These tax shelters are condoned by the CRA and certainly have income tax benefits, but also have investment risk. In simple terms, you purchase an FTLP for say $5,000, obtain an income tax deduction for $5,000, and then have a mutual fund of small cap resource stocks with a nil cost base that you can sell two years hence. People become so enamoured with the income tax savings that they don't realize they have overallocated their portfolio to risky small-cap resource stocks (I call these people "tax shelter junkies"). In some cases, in the ultimate irony, they purchase such a large amount of FTLP that they create alternative minimum tax, defeating their original intent of saving on income taxes.

Now, let's look at some probate misplanning:

Probate taxes in Ontario are, for all intents and purposes, 1.5% of your estate upon death. Yet people blindly transfer stock investments to their children to avoid these taxes. These people are very pleased with themselves, as they have saved 1.5% in probate fees; however, their chest-thumping quickly seems to abate when I inform them they may now owe 23% capital gains tax on the deemed disposition they caused by transferring their investments to their children.

Many Canadians also commonly open a bank account with joint ownership and the right of survivorship with one of their children for ease of administration as they age and to avoid probate tax. The parent typically assumes that the monies in joint ownership belong to their estate, to be shared by all their children. However, the child they opened the account with often considers those funds to be theirs alone. Thus, the parent may have saved 1.5% in probate tax, but they also may have been the catalyst for litigation amongst their children.

In conclusion, care must be taken to ensure your income tax planning does not leave you barking up the wrong tree.

---

1 Canada Revenue Agency. "T4037 Capital Gains 2011." Canada Revenue Agency, Revised 2011. 7.

2 Ibid.

3 Canada Revenue Agency. "IT-128R Capital Cost Allowance – Depreciable Property." Canada Revenue Agency. Interpretation Bulletin IT-128R, 1985, s 4.

4 Tonn v. Canada (C.A.), [1996] 2 F.C. 73, at para 28.

Chapter 7

RRIFs and RRSPs - The Retirement Acronyms

RRIFs – How They Work and Tax Planning

By the end of the year in which you turn 71, you are required to terminate your Registered Retirement Savings Plan ("RRSP"). You have three viable options at that point:

1. You can transfer your RRSP savings into a Registered Retirement Income Fund ("RRIF").

2. You can transfer your funds into an annuity.

3. You can blend the RRIF and annuity option.

There is a fourth option, which is to withdraw the full value of your RRSP; however, unless you have a very small RRSP, this option is a non-starter.

The RRIF Rules

RRIFs are subject to an annual minimum withdrawal, which commences the year after you open your RRIF account. The minimum withdrawal amounts are based on a percentage of the value of your RRIF. The standard percentages are noted below:

Age*	RRIFs established after 1992	Age*	RRIFs established after 1992
71	7.38%	83	9.58%
72	7.48%	84	9.93%
73	7.59%	85	10.33%
74	7.71%	86	10.79%
75	7.85%	87	11.33%
76	7.99%	88	11.96%
77	8.15%	89	12.71%
78	8.33%	90	13.62%
79	8.53%	91	14.73%
80	8.75%	92	16.12%
81	8.99%	93	17.92%
82	9.27%	94 or older	20.00%
* On January 1 of the year for which the minimum amount is being calculated.			

The minimum withdrawal rates may force you to withdraw more funds than you need to live, and push you into a higher income tax bracket. Fortunately, you can elect to have the withdrawal minimums based on the age of a younger spouse or common-law partner. This election cannot be changed once you select the spousal age option.

If you have a spouse under the age of 71, the minimum percentage is calculated as 1 divided by (90 minus your spouse's age). For example, if your spouse is only 50, you would only have to withdraw 2.5% [1/ (90-50)].

The website *RetirementAdvisor.ca* has an excellent RRIF calculator to help you determine your minimum withdrawal rates and whether you should use your age or your spouse's.

Income Tax Planning for RRSPs and RRIFs before Age 71

It may make sense to withdraw funds from your RRSP before you convert it to an RRIF at age 71. You would only do this where your marginal income tax rate will be lower in the years between retirement and when you convert your RRSP at age 71. For example, assume you will have $40,000 of pension and investment income when you retire at age 65. At this level of income, the next $4,000 you earn will be taxed at approximately 24%, and the following $27,000 will be taxed at 31%. Thus, you may want to cash in $4,000 (and possibly more), since when you must withdraw funds from your RRIF at age 72, you will at minimum be taxed at 31% (or possibly higher, depending upon your minimum RRIF withdrawal and your ability to pension-split with your spouse).

You also want to manage your total net income so that you will not have to pay back your Old Age Security ("OAS"). The 2014 clawback threshold starts at $71,592 with your OAS being completely clawed-back once your total net income reaches $115,716.

To some, the above may seem simplistic and fairly standard advice. In fact, I was taken to task by a reader for similar advice during my six-part series on retirement (See Chapter 9). The reader commented that they "have seen very few models that give a detailed picture of how to manage the drawdown of your RRSP and take into account the minimum RRIF withdrawals." As I like a challenge, I actually attempted to create such a model. Alas, after a couple hours and a brief discussion with Michael James (the writer behind the blog Michael James on Money who is a math whiz), I realized this is a herculean task in which I have little interest in attempting to conquer. Thus, I suggest the only way to deal with this issue is to have your financial planner consider your RRSP drawdown in context of your retirement plan.

As RRIF withdrawals at age 65 and beyond qualify as pension income, they will be eligible for the $2,000 pension income tax credit. Many advisors suggest converting a small portion of your RRSP into a RRIF so that you can claim the pension credit. The pension credit is worth approximately $400 on a $2,000 RRIF withdrawal. Keep in mind you may have to pay an administration fee for your RRIF that could offset some of this benefit.

If you will have earned income in the year of retirement, say 2014, you can make an RRSP over-contribution in December 2014 (equal to 18% of your 2014 earned income). This will allow you to claim a 2015 RRSP deduction. You will pay a one-month over-contribution penalty of 1% for your December over-contribution; however your RRSP over-contribution will cease January 1, 2015 (e.g. if your 2014 earned income is $100,000, you can make a $18,000 over-contribution in December 2014. You will owe a $180 penalty, but can deduct the $18,000 RRSP contribution on your 2015 return even though your RRSP is now an RRIF).

If you have a younger spouse and you have RRSP contribution room, you can contribute to a spousal RRSP up to and including the year in which they turn 71.

Most people know they must convert their RRSP to an RRIF by the end of their 71st year, but give no heed to any planning before the year of conversion. As noted above, tax planning should begin with your RRSP/RRIF in your early- to mid-sixties.

[Author's Note: The 2015 Federal budget proposes to lower the minimum RRIF withdrawal limits.]

The Kid in the Candy Store: Human Nature, RRSPs, Free Cash, and the Holy Grail

Some time ago I read a column by Rob Carrick of *The Globe and Mail* titled *Why TFSAs trump RRSPs for the young and lower paid.*[1] The column was premised on a paper by Jamie Golombek of CIBC on why Tax-Free Savings Accounts ("TFSAs") beat RRSPs as a better retirement savings vehicle for some Canadians.[2] This topic has subsequently been beaten to death, so I just want to concentrate on the exchange I had with Jamie regarding human nature and its impact on investing.

The Globe and Mail had an online discussion about the above article and I sent in the following comment: "The problem with technically correct solutions is that they ignore human nature. As a chartered professional accountant, I can tell you people consider their RRSPs holy and try their best to never withdraw from them. A TFSA or any accessible account is like candy, you stare and stare and then indulge."

Jamie responded "You may be surprised to learn that that 80% of all RRSP withdrawals are made by individuals under age 60, generally pre-retirement! Not much of a holy grail!" Jamie's paper also reports that recent data shows 1.9 million Canadians withdrew $9.3 billion from their RRSPs in 2008, and taken in conjunction with the 80% withdrawal statistic noted above, suggests RRSP funds are being used well before retirement age to supplement income.[3]

Jamie clearly considered the human nature aspect of investing in his report, and provides statistics to develop or support the thesis of his paper. I have no issue with his statistics or his assertion that RRSPs are being used to supplement retirement income by those under the age of 60. I do object, however, to his contention that RRSPs are not considered the holy grail.

In my practice, I have observed that RRSPs are the holy grail for most of my clients. More importantly, RRSPs seem to act like those invisible fences for dogs and form a barrier to prevent my clients from "grabbing" at them; although I think Jamie would suggest the barrier may have some holes in it based on his statistics.

I asked Rob Carrick his thoughts on the matter and he responded, "I'm stunned every time I read stats on how many people take money out of their RRSPs, never mind TFSAs. The harder it is to withdraw from a retirement savings vehicle, the better."

On the surface, it is difficult to refute Jamie's assertion without my own statistics. Numbers are numbers. But if we could dig a little deeper, the same numbers may tell a different story. Here is where human nature and its impact on investing come into play. Human nature, like physical nature, takes the path of least resistance. At the end of the day, my observation of human nature takes me down the same road as Rob: the greater the barrier, the better – even if some ignore the barrier. Anyway, I will leave this for the psychologists to study and will return to my laboratory (my office), and provide some personal experiences on human nature and free cash.

RRSPs: The Holy Grail, or Just Full of Holes?

In my accounting practice, it has been my experience, based on discussions with my clients, that they withdraw RRSPs almost exclusively for financial need only, and not for discretionary purposes. I will concede that my clients' incomes are well above the national average, and thus they may not be a representative sample. If we could somehow ask each person who withdraws funds from their RRSP in Canada, "Why are you doing such and what is the intended use of the funds?", I am convinced that the vast majority would answer, "We are taking out the funds due to financial need and not for discretionary purchases." Most people take a certain pride and comfort in their RRSP savings.

There is a peculiar permanency in investing in an RRSP that is not nearly as tangible in a TFSA or other savings account. Non-RRSP savings accounts seem to represent "leftover money". RRSPs represent security against old age impoverishment. That is the holy grail. Most people cash out RRSPs only under financial duress. Financial duress is not the same as supplementing income.

So what about those alarmingly counterintuitive statistics that would suggest we have become an unholy nation desecrating their RRSPs? In my humble opinion, it is highly probable that many Canadians are convinced that they have to contribute to RRSPs by the various advertisements they are bombarded with in January and February each year by financial institutions, and at the urging of financial commentators, when in fact, many were really not in a position to contribute to their RRSP in the first place (thus dooming their RRSP from inception and inflating the withdrawal statistics).

I See It, I Want It

Now, assuming we are not compelled to withdraw our savings (or perhaps more aptly, borrowings), restricted savings accounts are like invisible fences, or the glass in front of the candy counter. Withdrawing cash from an accessible savings account like a TFSA is relatively easy, especially when we see that cash as "leftover earnings", or as a well-deserved reward for how much we've earned or how hard we've worked. If we move away from restricted accounts such as RRSPs, the invisible fence seems to turn off. Now the buying is easy; self-restraint is hard. Accessible cash quickly winds its way along the path of least resistance and to a cash register.

I often observe the sweet lure of accessible cash in the actions of many self-employed individuals and professionals with respect to their quarterly personal income tax installments. Some make significant sums of money, but you would not believe how many don't have the funds to pay their quarterly income tax installments. This results in huge income tax liabilities around April 30th and installment interest and penalties for failure to make these required installment payments. Why don't they have this cash you ask? In some cases they have not collected their accounts receivable or received allocations from their partnerships, but in many cases, they have spent the free cash that should have been allocated to their income tax installments on discretionary items only because it was easily accessible and winking at them.

A hot topic that has been widely debated is whether it is better for small business owners to eschew salary and RRSPs in favour of leaving the funds in their holding company. Technically, leaving the money in the corporation is correct (although I have some reservations with this strategy because you stop RRSP contributions, lose eligibility for Canada Pension Plan income in the future, and potentially forgo the deductibility of child care expenses if no salary is taken). In my opinion, the candy (i.e. available cash) will prove too tempting for most people, and some of those corporate funds will find their way to cover that vacation they wanted in Europe, or that new car or boat they have their eye on; whereas if those funds were contributed to an RRSP, the invisible fence effect would come into play. I have observed this firsthand with the typical current holding company structure, where excess profits from an operating company are moved to the holding company; this new twist would only create more accessible cash to potentially be withdrawn. However, if you are disciplined, leaving profits in your corporation rather than making RRSP contributions may often make sense.

Intuitively Rationally Irrational

Although not directly related to free cash, an example of personal behavior superseding fundamental financial common sense is in relation to income tax refunds. Individuals can file form *T1213* to obtain waivers to reduce income tax withholdings in certain circumstances, but almost no one does. Ignoring the administrative issue of obtaining the income tax withholding reduction (which may contribute in part), individuals just love their lump sum tax refunds (usually as result of their RRSP contributions), and they intuitively know they would not save an amount equal to the same lump sum income tax refund if they had their income tax withholding reduced on a bi-weekly or semi-monthly basis.

I have only anecdotal evidence to prove people consider their RRSPs the holy grail. But really, is it unreasonable to accept that TFSAs or other non-registered accounts are merely shelves displaying the cash-candy to which our sweet tooth cash-cravings will inevitably succumb? The path of least resistance generally ends at the cash register in the candy store. The high road is easier to follow when the candy case is locked. A financial vehicle that people feel is "locked in" will help stymie our natural inclination to self-indulge and spend, and will only be accessed under financial duress and not necessarily as a supplement to retirement income. Now that is a holy grail indeed.

---

1 Carrick, Rob. "Why TFSAs Trump RRSPs for the Young and Lower-paid." The Globe and Mail. January 13, 2011.
2 Golombek, Jamie. "Blinded by the "Refund": Why TFSAs May Beat RRSPs as Better Retirement Savings Vehicle for Some Canadians." CIBC. January, 2011.
3 Ibid., 5.

Chapter 8

Family Assets – Dividing, Sharing and Taxing

How Your Family Dynamic Can Affect Your Estate Planning

Estate planning is a complicated and delicate process. When you have more than one child, the planning process is full of mines; some are in clear sight, but many are hidden. Parents have to navigate these minefields with respect to the determination of executors, the distribution of family heirlooms, and the distribution of hard assets. The above decisions may be impacted by the financial wherewithal of your children, your relationship with your children's spouses, your grandchildren (or lack thereof), and in some cases, favouritism of certain children.

The above are what I call vertical family hierarchy issues. These are issues resulting from parents making decisions that will affect their children, and potentially the way their children will view their parents after death.

What parents do not often consider is how these vertical decisions impact horizontally, i.e. how the interrelationship of your children must be considered in your estate planning. Any parent who does not consider these relationships runs the risk of creating a divisive wedge between their children, as sibling rivalry and jealousies may rear their ugly heads.

I will attempt to identify several estate planning issues that not only have vertical consequences, but also have horizontal consequences that require parents to consider their children's relationships in context of their planning.

The Family Business

Where there is a family business and the succession plan is to pass on the business to the next generation, several issues must be considered. The issues include the following:

How many children have an interest in the family business?

If you have more than one child, is one specific child best suited to the role of CEO or president? If so, based on your children's current relationships, do you foresee them working well together, butting heads, or worse? If the eldest child is named president, have you reinforced the perception the younger child has held for years that the eldest is favoured and always assumed the most capable?

How do you value the business?

This is not an issue if all the children are given equal shares of the business, since they will have equal ownership no matter the actual value attributed to the company. But what if you decide to leave the business to one child and equalize the other child(ren) with cash or other assets? The value of the business can fluctuate wildly over the years, with the result being that the child who inherits the shares may in essence have inherited a significantly larger asset than the other child(ren). Alternatively, the shares of the company may prove to be worth substantially less than the assets distributed to the other child(ren) if business conditions cause the value of the business to diminish. As a parent, can you do anything to avoid potential disparities in value? I have seen situations where asset distributions were equal at the time of death, but the inherited business grew astronomically, and the children who did not inherit the company shares felt wronged by their parents.

Finally, if you have undertaken an estate freeze while alive (see Chapter 12 on introducing a family trust as a shareholder and the related discussion on estate freezes), which child will inherit the voting shares? You risk alienating the children who do not receive the voting shares, since they may feel that you did not think they had enough acumen to vote and run the company.

The Family Cottage

The family cottage is often a contentious asset. In some families all the children want to keep ownership of the cottage, and in others only one or two siblings want the cottage. As a parent, you must speak to your children and determine who wants the cottage. Where more than one child wants the cottage, you have to consider whether those children have a good relationship, and if they will be able to share ownership without starting a world war. If not, do you have to consider selling the cottage in your later years to avoid creating a divisive issue amongst your children?

Another important factor to consider is whether the children interested in keeping the cottage have the financial wherewithal to pay their share of the cottages expenses on a yearly basis. If not, how do you overcome this potential issue (especially if one child has the financial resources and another does not)?

Also, where there is a large inherent gain on the cottage, you have to determine whether your estate will be able to pay the income taxes without forcing a sale of the cottage and causing the estate to unwind your original intention to keep the cottage in the family. In this case, you may be able to use life insurance to cover off this issue.

The Will

A will may be construed as a document that reflects a parent's opinion of their children and confirms the children's opinions of themselves. If you infer one child is more responsible than the others (by selecting certain children as executors and excluding others), you risk igniting the fire of past resentments amongst the children and potentially causing resentment of you, even in death.

Assuming you can navigate the determination of the executor(s) amongst your children without creating jealousy or animosity (if not, a corporate executor may be required), how do you distribute your assets upon death in a manner that mitigates any damage that can occur to your children's relationships?

The distribution of material items is fraught with danger. How does one ever balance sentimentality and value? If you provide one child a sentimental heirloom, you risk that child complaining the other children got more value, while the other children complain they were not left sentimental heirlooms. What if you have art? How do you balance the value of art that have significant value differentials?

What about a situation where one child has been financially successful and another has not? If your will provides for a greater distribution to the child with less money, how do you ensure you do not create resentment with the financially well-off child? The less well-off child, who should be ecstatic, may actually be insulted, as they can interpret the larger inheritance as their parents saying they were "financial losers" as opposed to being grateful for the larger inheritance. In these cases, one must tread carefully, but an unequal allocation may be more readily accepted when you explain your reasoning to your children before your death.

Another issue is grandchildren. Where the number of grandchildren is different in each family or one child does not have any family, do you give equal amounts to each family or equal amounts per child? How about where one of your children may be incapable of providing for a grandchild's education and you feel a trust would be appropriate? Will any consideration other than equal consideration be construed as favouritism by your children?

Finally, many parents have provided loans to their children to assist with university, purchasing a house, or what have you. How do you deal with prior gifts or loans? If you forgive the loans, you may have an unequal distribution and cause an issue amongst your children. Thus, you may want to consider a reduction of any distributions in the will for any outstanding loans.

This whole discussion may be construed as ludicrous on a certain level. Some may say this is why they will not leave anything to their children. Others may say "I will leave my children whatever I feel like and if the distribution is unequal, so be it." However, it has been my experience that the majority of parents truly do not want to create any dissension amongst their children and aim to provide for an equal distribution. Even though they will have passed on, many parents still don't want to alienate any of their children or cause resentment upon their death.

A Family Vacation – A Memory Worth Not Dying for

I am a proponent of providing partial gifts while alive if you have the financial resources. My rationale is simple: why not receive the pleasure of your gift either directly (such as a family vacation) or vicariously (by observing your children or grandchildren enjoy their gift such as a bike, car, or even a cottage)?

The concept of a partial gift being used, at least in part, for a family vacation has substantial appeal to many parents. A family vacation is appealing because a parent can participate in the experience, the vacation (more often than not) results in memories that last a lifetime for all the participants, and lastly, the parent has control over the gift.

I can attest personally to the benefits of a family vacation. Several years ago, my in-laws funded a Disney Cruise vacation for their children, their children's spouses, and their grandchildren. This trip had a profound impact on the bonding of the grandchildren. In the case of my in-laws, the memories and enhancement of their grandchildren's relationships were priceless and continue to this day.

Another very poignant and moving example of the gift of travel is the story of Les Brooks. Les, a Vietnam veteran, had unresolved issues relating to the war, and as he states in a Princess Cruises travel blog, "Vietnam was a place I left in 1966 praying I would never have to go back. But Christle sensed the deeper truth...I was curious about the place; I wanted and needed to see for myself what life was like today for the people of a country that I left so torn apart by war."[1]

One day during the course of a conversation, Les' mother asked him that if he could take a trip anywhere in the world, where would he go. After thinking about the question, he surprised his mother by saying

Vietnam. Unbeknownst to Les, she later booked him on a cruise to Vietnam.

Sadly, his mother passed away before Les took the cruise and could not observe the impact this gift had on her son's life, but I would surmise she knew the impact it would have, as she paid for the cruise. While Les' gift was not a family bonding vacation, it was a gift provided while his mother was alive, a trip that may never have occurred if Les inherited the money and spent it otherwise.

The concept of using a partial gift to fund a family vacation has become popular for both family bonding and financial reasons. While many parents often have money, their children do not as they are establishing careers and families. Many parents want their children and grandchildren to enjoy their lives and as such, decide to fund family vacations so they can enjoy it with them.

I have observed the family vacation phenomenon on several of my own vacations. Suddenly a horde of people arrive at the pool or restaurant (not necessarily a welcome sight for other vacationers) with corny matching t-shirts saying "Smith Family Vacation 2014", or some other similar sentiment.

Although we all know that any large family gathering can veer off the rails, these trips often bridge the generation gap between offspring and grandparents and parents. I often hear people reference these types of family vacations when they have a family get-together, or when the topic arises over dinner with non-family members.

Personally, I would rather hear my grandchildren say (or know they are saying) "When I was young, my grandparents took me on the most amazing trip!" than "I just inherited $25,000 from my grandparents, what should I buy with it?"

Probate Fee Planning – Income Tax, Estate, and Legal Issues to Consider

Planning to reduce or eliminate probate taxes requires one to navigate a minefield of income tax rules, joint tenancy and right of survivorship issues, and legal precedents. Questions of legal vs. beneficial ownership of property and evidence of intention often come into play. The scary thing is that this type of planning is often done by the uninformed. After reading this, I hope it becomes clear to you that you need to consult a tax or estate lawyer when undertaking any significant probate planning.

Probate Fees in Ontario

In Ontario, probate fees (technically called "estate administration tax") are levied on a deceased taxpayer's estate at the rate of $250 on the first $50,000 of assets, and $15 per $1,000 thereafter. Consequently, if a person were to die with assets of $1,000,000, the estate would have a probate fee liability of $14,500. An estate of $5,000,000 would have a probate fee liability of $74,500. The other provinces have varying probate fee regimes.

Two of the more common strategies to minimize probate fees are making gifts and transferring assets to joint tenancy. While these techniques may reduce or eliminate probate fees, they can create significant income tax and estate issues if not done properly.

Gifts to Children and Your Spouse

If cash gifts are made during a person's lifetime, they will reduce the value of his or her estate for probate purposes. If the gift is made to a child under 18 years of age, the income earned on the gifted property (i.e. interest and dividends) will be attributed back to the person making the gift for income tax purposes. Where a cash gift is made to a spouse, the income earned on these assets (i.e. interest and dividends, as well as capital gains and losses) is attributed back to the person making the gift for income tax purposes. Cash gifts made to children who have attained the age of 18 do not invoke the income attribution rules in the *Income Tax Act*, so you can make a gift to an 18-year-old child which will reduce probate fees and not create any income tax problems.

Where non-cash gifts of capital property (such as gold or stocks) are made to a person other than your spouse, the property is deemed to be sold at its fair market value ("FMV") for income tax purposes. Thus, if a mother were to gift 1,000 shares of BCE having a total cost of $10,000 and FMV of $30,000 to her 20-year-old son, she would realize a capital gain for income tax purposes of $20,000, even though the shares were not sold and no money was received.

In an effort to avoid probate fees, some families seek to add the names of children to the title of a surviving parent's home. This is done by transferring the title to the house from the surviving parent ("original owner") to the children and surviving parent as joint tenants (the "new owners"). Upon the transfer, the original owner/parent is treated for income tax purposes as having sold a portion of the transferred house based on the number of new owners. For example, if the new owners were a parent and two children, each new owner would be treated as owning a one-third interest. This means the original owner/parent in this example will be considered to have disposed of a two-thirds interest in the house. The two-thirds sale would be tax-free due to the principal residence exemption. However, two-thirds of any increase in value from the date of the gift until the house is ultimately sold will not be eligible for the principal residence exemption (assuming that the children have their own principal residences). If you are into horror stories, check out Jim Yih's blog for a nightmare of a story of a parent that put a child on the title to her principal residence.[2]

Situations such as the above may be avoided in certain circumstances where a lawyer knowledgeable in tax and/or estate law separates legal from beneficial ownership before the transfer. The Canada Revenue Agency ("CRA") has stated that where there is a change in legal ownership without a corresponding change in the beneficial ownership (the real value is in beneficial ownership), there is no disposition of the asset for tax purposes.[3] What could be accomplished in the above scenario is a transfer of legal title only, without changing beneficial ownership. This would have no income tax implications but would assist in dealing with probate issues.

A further problem with transfers to joint tenancy (such as the home above) arises because with a joint tenancy, the entire title will pass to the last person alive (which often is not the intent of the parent). For example, if a bank account belonging to Mom is transferred into a new account in the names of Mom, Son, and Daughter as joint tenants with right of survivorship, and Mom and Son die together, Daughter would become the "owner" of the entire account. This was not likely the intent of Mom, who probably wanted to split the account between her two children (or her grandchildren, if one of her children passed away). If not for trying to save probate fees, Mom would have never done this.

Joint Tenancy Can Be Problematic – the Pecore Case

If property is held as joint tenants with a right of survivorship, on its face, the property will pass automatically to the surviving joint owner and is therefore not subject to probate fees. I have seen many cases where parents put their adult children's names on bank accounts and investment portfolio accounts. The parents consider these accounts to now be exempt from probate, yet the parent continues to report the income earned on these investments in their own name for income tax purposes. (As noted above, it is the CRA's view that if beneficial ownership has not changed, there is no disposition for income tax purposes, which is in accordance with the parents' plan above. However, at least from the CRA's perspective, they have some issues with whether probate transfer is effective, which is not in accordance with the parents' plan above.) However, many parents fail to look past the probate issue and their intention in regard to the funds is unclear. Is it the parents' intention that the funds held jointly with one child belong to that child, or do they belong to all their children, and there is an understanding that the child on the account will share with their siblings?

This issue was addressed in *Pecore v Pecore*, a 2007 Supreme Court case where the court addressed these two potentially conflicting intentions. Legally, these two intentions are known as the presumption of resulting trust and the presumption of advancement. The presumption of resulting trust means that when a parent dies, the transferred assets form part of their estate and will be passed on to the beneficiaries of the will (typically all their children). The presumption of advancement presumes any transfer to a specific child belongs to that child. The potential for conflict is rife where a parent transfers assets into joint tenancy with one child for ease of administration.

In the *Pecore* decision, the Supreme Court stated that where assets are transferred without consideration (such as to a child to avoid probate), the presumption of resulting trust will operate in almost all cases (save transfers from a parent to a minor child). This means that where a parent transfers assets into a joint account with one child, there must be evidence of the intention to make a gift to that specific child.[4] As I am not a lawyer, I cannot state what counts as refutable evidence, but from what I have read, a written document is a minimum requirement.

If done correctly and carefully, gifting, creating joint tenancy arrangements, and separating legal from beneficial ownership can result in the reduction or elimination of probate fees. However, probate planning can lead to unintended income tax and estate implications (as discussed above) that far outweigh the probate tax savings. It is essential that you engage a lawyer who is comfortable in dealing with these issues (usually a tax or estate lawyer) when undertaking any significant probate planning.

Transferring Property among Family Members – A Potential Income Tax Nightmare

Transfers of property among family members often create significant income tax issues and can be either errors of commission or errors of omission. Over my 25 years as an accountant, I have been referred some unbelievably messed-up situations involving intrafamilial transfers of property. Most of these referrals have come about because someone has read an article and decided they are now probate experts, real estate lawyers, or tax lawyers.

Transfers of Property – Why They Are Undertaken

Many individuals transfer capital property (real estate and common shares being the most common) in and amongst their family like hot cakes. Some of the reasons people undertake these transfers are: (1) the transferor has creditor issues and believes that if certain properties are transferred, the properties will become creditor-protected; (2) the transferor wishes to reduce probate fees on his or her death; and (3) the transferor wishes to either gift the property, transfer beneficial title, or income split with lower-income family members.

I will not discuss the first reason because it is legal in nature, but be aware, section 160(1) of the *Income Tax Act* can make you legally responsible for the transferor's income tax liability[5], and there may be fraudulent conveyance issues amongst other matters.

Transfers of Property – Income Tax Implications

When a property is transferred without consideration (i.e. as a gift or just transferred to another person's name), the transferor is generally deemed to have sold the property for proceeds equal to its FMV. If the property has increased in value since the time the transferor first acquired it, a capital gain will be realized and there will be taxes to be paid even though ownership of the property has stayed within the family. For example, if Mom owns a rental property worth $500,000 which she purchased for $100,000 and she transfers it to her daughter, Mom is deemed to have a $400,000 capital gain, even though she did not receive any money.

There is one common exception to the deemed disposition rule: the *Income Tax Act* permits transfers between spouses to take place at the transferor's adjusted cost base ("ACB") instead of at the FMV of the capital property.[6]

This difference is best illustrated by an example: Mary owns shares of Bell Canada which she purchased five years ago at $50. The FMV of the shares today is $75. If Mary transferred the shares of Bell Canada to her brother, Bob, she would realize a capital gain of $25. If instead Mary transferred the shares of Bell Canada to her husband, Doug, the shares would be transferred at Mary's ACB of $50 and no capital gain would be realized. It must be noted that if Doug sells the shares in the future, Mary would be required to report the capital gain realized at that time (i.e. the proceeds Doug receives from selling the shares, less Mary's original cost of $50), as well as any dividends received by Doug on those shares from the date of transfer.

As noted in the example above, when transfers are made to spouses or children who are minors (under the age of 18), the income attribution rules can apply, and any income generated by the transferred properties is attributed back to the transferor (the exception being that there is no attribution on capital gains earned by a minor). The application of this rule is reflected in that Mary must report the capital gain and any dividends received by Doug. If the transferred property is sold, there is often attribution even on the substituted property.

We have discussed that when property is transferred to a non-arm's-length person, the vendor is deemed to have sold the property at its FMV. However, what happens when the non-arm's-length person has paid no consideration (or consideration less than), the FMV? The answer is that in all cases other than gifts, bequests, and inheritances, the transferees' cost is the amount they actually paid for the property and there is no adjustment to FMV, a very punitive result.

In English, what these last two sentences are saying is that if you legally gift something, the cost base and proceeds of disposition are the FMV. For example, if your brother pays you $5,000 for shares worth $50,000, you will be deemed to sell the shares for $50,000, but your brother's cost will now only be $5,000; whereas if you gifted the shares, his cost base would be $50,000. A strange result, considering he actually paid you. This generally results in "double taxation" when the property is ultimately sold by the transferee (your brother, in this case), as you were deemed to sell at $50,000, and your brother's gain is measured from only $5,000 (and not the FMV of $50,000).

Transfers of a Principal Residence – the Ultimate Potential Tax Nightmare

I have seen several cases where a parent decides to change the ownership of his or her principal residence such that it is to be held jointly by the parent and one or more of their children. In the case of a parent changing ownership of, say, half of their principal residence to one of their children, the parent is deemed to have disposed of half of the property. This initial transfer is tax-free, since it is the parent's principal residence. However, *a transfer into joint ownership can often create an unforeseen tax problem when the property is eventually sold*. Subsequent to the change in ownership, the child will own half the principal residence. When the property is eventually sold, the gain realized by the parent on his or her half of the property is exempt from tax since it qualifies for the principal residence exemption; however, since the child now owns half of the property, the child is subject to tax on any capital gain realized on their half of the property (50% of the difference between the sale price and the FMV at the time the parent transferred the property to the child, assuming the child has a principal residence of their own).

Many people are far too cavalier when transferring property among family members. It should be clear by now that extreme care should be taken before transferring any real estate, shares, or investments to a family member. I strongly urge you to consult with your accountant or to engage an accountant when contemplating a family transfer.

---

1 Brooks, Les. "My Mother's Gift of Healing." InspiredtoCruise.com. March 20, 2012.

2 Yih, Jim. "Use Caution before Putting Your Kids on Title of Your Principal Residence." Retire Happy.

3 Income Tax Act, RSC 1985, c 1 (5th Supp), s 248(1)

4 Pecore v. Pecore, [2007] 1 SCR 795.

5 Income Tax Act, s 160(1)

6 Ibid., s 74.2(1)

Chapter 9

Retirement – How to Avoid Eating Alpo

How Much Money do I Need to Retire? Heck if I Know or Anyone Else Does!

Part 1

A six-part series dealing with retirement withdrawal rates, studies by retirement experts, and some numbers.

Let's be honest; no one knows how much money they really need to retire. My own attempts to quantify my "retirement number" result in a range of hundreds of thousands of dollars. Unless you fancy yourself a two-headed economist/soothsayer, you can only plan based on historical investment returns, anticipated spending requirements, and assumed inflation rates. That does not even account for wild cards such as your longevity, or the random sequence of returns you will get from the stock market. The best-laid retirement plans of mice and men can often go awry... when bam – you get a sudden economic shock or stock market aberration and your retirement plan becomes as worthless as the paper you wrote it on (those of a cynical nature have been known to say that all any retirement plan proves is ink sticks to paper).

I've been pondering this question for over a year as I have attempted to figure out the nest egg I need to fund my own retirement. My final conclusion: the financial and economic variables you need to consider to even attempt to answer this question are staggering (I detail these in Part 5 of this series), and I will never come to a definitive answer. This realization is actually liberating, yet frightening. Liberating, as I realize the best I can do is to create a plan that is based on a framework of historical data, actual data, and my best guess estimates. Frightening, in the sense that I may not know until it's too late if I have grievously miscalculated my retirement needs. While going through this nest egg building process, I made some notes and read various papers. I soon realized I had a six-part series.

For some, this series may be far too detailed. For others, the discussion will provide food for thought. For the mathematicians and academics out there, the discussion will not be "academic" enough (although the problem with many academic papers is that only the author and other retirement/mathematical experts understand what the heck they are proposing). However, in all cases, despite the difficulty I see in making a definitive determination of how much money you or I need to retire, burying your head in the sand and ignoring the issue is not an option. It is imperative you try and at least get a ballpark number for planning purposes, and continuously refine that number over time. I hope this series will provide you the impetus to plan for your own retirement if you have not yet done so.

So where does one start? The 4% withdrawal rule is one of the most commonly accepted rule-of-thumb retirement strategies. Simply put, the rule says that if you have an equally-balanced portfolio of stocks and bonds, you should be able to withdraw 4% of your retirement savings each year (adjusted for inflation), and those savings will last for 30-35 years.

If you embrace this rule of thumb, then in theory you should be able to determine how much money you will need at retirement by working backwards. Unfortunately, it is not quite that simple; the 4% withdrawal rule has some inherent flaws which I discuss below, and therefore should only be used as part of your retirement framework to provide you an idea of what would be a sustainable nest egg.

Whether the withdrawal percentage is reduced from 4% to 2%, or you modify the formula, everyone is still searching for the holy grail of retirement planning, with the big question: *What is your safe withdrawal rate* (i.e. how much money can you safely withdraw from your nest egg each year and not run out of money before you pass away)?

Some retirement experts feel the search for a safe constant withdrawal rate is foolhardy, especially where you use a predetermined set rate.

Notwithstanding these concerns (which I believe have validity), because of the simplicity of the calculation, many people and financial institutions still feel the 4% rule is an excellent starting point in the determination of your retirement nest egg if you understand its limitations and flaws. I agree that this rule is simple to apply and understand, and thus over the next few parts, I will discuss various studies and papers that deal with the determination of a safe withdrawal rate and whether 4% is a safe withdrawal rate in this day and age. Finally, I will discuss variations of the rule put forth by retirement experts to adjust/correct for the perceived flaws of the rule of thumb.

Limitations of the 4% Rule

Some of the criticisms of the 4% model include:

1. The model does not account for income taxes on non-registered accounts and registered accounts.

2. The model does not account for transaction fees or management fees related to your investments.

3. The model treats everyone exactly the same.

4. The data for the model was based on only historical US stock data and does not include foreign equity data.

5. The model builds in an inflation adjustment; however some commentators feel the cumulative inflation adjustment may force you to make larger and larger withdrawals.

A Tax-Centric Variation on the 4% Withdrawal Rule

As result of the omissions above, especially the income tax component, I created a very crude tax-centric variation of the 4% rule to provide an alternative comparison to some of the other retirement formulas I discuss in Part 6. (Please note I said crude and tax-centric. I do not have the qualifications, let alone the time, to run statistical simulations to come up with a unique formula that, like every other formula, will be flawed because of the unquantifiable variables that must be considered in determining your retirement number.)

Now that I have dampened your expectations for my crude variation, I simply determined my spending requirements in retirement and subtracted from my spending requirement my estimated sources of retirement income (Old Age Security ["OAS"], Canada Pension Plan ["CPP"], etc.), which resulted in a retirement withdrawal shortfall.

Here is where my calculation gets tax-centric. I first calculate the income tax owing on my total estimated retirement income. This tax liability causes my retirement shortfall to increase. The next calculation is a bit circular, but I then come up with a revised withdrawal amount that after-tax covers my anticipated spending shortfall.

I then divide my required retirement after-tax withdrawal above by 4% (3% for a conservative approach), which tells me how much money outside of any CPP, OAS, or company pension (which I don't have) I need to accumulate for retirement. When I post actual numbers in Part 6 this will be much easier to follow and make a little more sense.

This crude estimate will give mathematicians heart palpitations. I know this tax-centric variation does not address multiple issues, but bear with me until you see where I go with this in Part 6.

In no way should you rely on this framework as the sole determinant for your own retirement planning. However, as you will see in Part 6, this number is not that far off from what I get when I have a financial planner use his software to provide me with "a number", and the number I get when I compare it to some other calculations suggested by retirement experts.

I Feel like a Lawyer with All These Caveats

One final caveat before I discuss some data and analysis. Please be aware that I am not a retirement expert, financial planner, mathematician (I dropped statistics in university), or psychic; and understand this series should not be construed as specific personal retirement planning advice. The intention of this series is to:

- summarize prior research (the information is overwhelming and the arguments made by some brilliant people, hard to disprove)

- assist you in determining your safe withdrawal rate percentage or provide you with an alternative method to the constant withdrawal methodology

- share my thought processes in trying to determine my own retirement needs

Hopefully all this will provide you with a launching point to help you consider what may be a reasonable retirement nest egg and/or a reasonable spending amount for your retirement.

Part 2

In Part 1 I introduced the 4% rule, the most commonly accepted rule-of-thumb retirement strategy. In Part 2 I discuss the guideline and its development in greater detail. As noted in Part 1, some retirement experts feel the rule is misleading and a terrible rule. I hope by the time you finish reading this series, you will have your own opinion on the 4% rule.

Conventional Wisdom – The 4% Withdrawal Rate

The 4% rule is a planning guideline for a sustainable rate of spending over a 30-year retirement. Years ago, a brilliant financial planner by the name of William P. Bengen (an MIT graduate of aeronautical engineering) got tired of being asked how much money his clients needed to retire, so he initiated a study that basically concluded that if you retire with a diversified portfolio split 50/50 between bonds and stocks, you will be able to safely withdraw 4% of the initial balance, plus an inflation-adjusted amount for the next 33 years and quite possibly as long as 50 years.[1]

For example, if you have $800,000 when you retire, under the 4% withdrawal rate you can take out $32,000 the first year. If inflation is 2%, your second year withdrawal amount will be $32,640 ($32,000 x 1.02). If inflation is 1.5% in your third year, your withdrawal will be $33,130 ($32,640 x 1.015), and so on. It is important to note that this is not a percentage of portfolio withdrawal method where you take the ending balance at the end of each year and draw 4%, but is a consistent withdrawal amount based on your original nest egg adjusted for inflation each year, which some experts find distasteful.

It should be noted that in a subsequent study, Mr. Bengen added US small-company stocks to the mix, which increased the portfolio's volatility and potential return. To adjust for this, he revised the with-drawal rule to 4.5%.[2] However, I will continue to use the more conservative 4% withdrawal amount for discussion purposes.

In a 2012 paper written by Mr. Bengen, he discusses some contingency planning, which includes potentially reducing spending and increasing income.[3]

Mr. Bengen did not provide a detailed summary of the market returns he used in his calculations, although he provided some returns for certain extrapolated years (10.3% for stocks, 5.1% for bonds, and 3% inflation).[4]

The Trinity Study – Support for the 4% Withdrawal Rate

A subsequent study, known as the Trinity Study, by Philip L. Cooley, Carl M. Hubbard and Daniel T. Walz supports Bengen's assertions. Some critics say this study supports Bengen because they use the same flawed data.

The Cooley, Hubbard, and Walz study produced a number of conclusions, including[5]:

- Early retirees who anticipate long payout periods should plan on lower withdrawal rates

- Bonds in the portfolio increase the success rate for low to mid-level withdrawal rates, but most retirees would benefit from allocating at least 50% to common stocks

- For stock-denominated portfolios, withdrawal rates of 3%-4% represent exceedingly conservative behaviour and will likely leave large estates

The authors comment that if history is any guide for the future, then withdrawal rates of 3%-4% are extremely unlikely to exhaust any portfolio of bonds and stocks (in almost any combination).

But what happens to your retirement planning if stock market history does not repeat itself? Poor stock market returns for the last few years (until 2013), countries defaulting or close to defaulting, historically low interest rates, and tough economic times have caused some pundits to say we are in different times and the 4% rule is outdated, as it only captures periods of great prosperity. In Part 3 of this series I discuss the various modern studies and reports on what is the proper withdrawal rate upon retirement.

MARK GOODFIELD

Part 3

In Parts 1 and 2, you read about the commonly accepted 4% withdrawal rule. This rule of thumb suggests that if you have an equally balanced portfolio of stocks and bonds, you should be able to withdraw 4% of your retirement savings each year adjusted for inflation, and those savings should last 30-35 years. In this part, I consider an alternative point of view, and then review modern studies and reports on how the 4% withdrawal rule is viewed in the context of market returns over the last decade.

Set Retirement Withdrawal Rates Should Never Be Used!

As noted earlier, some retirement experts do not like the 4% rule because it uses a constant spending amount and does not adjust to your evolving level of wealth. By shunning a set withdrawal rate, retirees may avoid spending shortfalls where their investments underperform and will not accumulate surpluses when they out-perform the market. My interpretation is that the experts feel you should spread your economic resources over your entire life, and that your spending rate and retirement withdrawal number should not be fixed to an arbitrary level, but that your spending rate should depend upon your personal preferences and your views on longevity risks.

Michael James

Before I move onto the modern safe withdrawal rate studies, I have to give a shout out to Michael James, a fellow Canadian personal finance blogger who created his own strategy, which includes holding five years of savings in a savings investment account. He uses his "Magic Number" calculator. The background to his calculator is discussed in his posts titled *A Retirement Income Strategy*, and *A Retirement Income Strategy Revisited*.

126

Modern Studies and Reports

The Bengen and Trinity studies, from which the 4% withdrawal rule originated, utilized stock market data from 1926 to 1976, and 1926 to 1995 respectively. Many commentators feel this historical data is no longer applicable in today's world.

To help you determine if 4% is a safe withdrawal rate for you (with the limitations I noted in Part 1), I've summarized below several current studies and reports on this topic. Some of the studies/reports continue to condone the 4% withdrawal rate, or are at least accepting of using a 4% withdrawal rate as a starting point. Others feel it is excessive and if you withdraw 4%, you will be eating cat food at some point in your retirement.

If you are like me, you will probably be overwhelmed by these reports, their arguments, and their data. Although you will never achieve certainty, your withdrawal percentage is the vital wildcard in trying to estimate your retirement nest egg, and you must draw a line in the sand using a percentage within your comfort zone, assuming you believe in a constant withdrawal rate strategy or a variation of the strategy.

The Studies That Suggest a 4% Withdrawal Is Still a Good Starting Point

What Charles Schwab has to Say

A report by Rob Williams, Director of Income Planning for the Schwab Center for Financial Research, says that Schwab suggests "the 4% rule as a starting point for planning purposes. Then, it's important to stay flexible as you spend in retirement."[6]

However, they go on to say that based on their current expectations for market returns over the next 30 years, Schwab calculates that a 3%

spending rate at the beginning of retirement may be more appropriate if you want to follow rigid spending rules, and ensure that your money will last.

What Vanguard has to Say

Revisiting the '4% spending rule', one of several excellent reports Vanguard has written over the years, states:

> For the majority of years from 1926 through 2011, the yield or income returns on a 50% stock/50% bond portfolio exceeded 4%. Over the last several decades, however, the yield for such a balanced portfolio has been steadily decreasing. At its peak, in 1982, the portfolio's average yield was 10.6%; by year-end 2011, the yield had dropped to 2.8%.[7]

Yet, Vanguard says that a 4% withdrawal rate is still a reasonable starting point. The report goes on to say:

> "a balanced 50% equity/50% bond portfolio for the decade ending 2021 are expected to center in the 3.0%-4.5% real-return range (Davis and Aliaga-Díaz, 2012)."[8]

Vanguard also has an excellent report on alternative spending strategies for those who are concerned that the constant 4% plus inflation adjusted amount in the rule of thumb may result in excessive withdrawals in poor performing markets. I will discuss that report in Part 4.

Part 4

In Part 3, I discussed modern studies that continue to view the 4% withdrawal rule as feasible in today's current environment. Now, I will look at various reports and studies by retirement experts who feel the 4% rule of thumb is excessive based on statistical simulations and the inclusion of worldwide market data, amongst other reasons. In addition, for those who feel a constant spending strategy is flawed whether the withdrawal rate is 2, 3, or 4%, I offer some alternative spending approaches.

The Naysayers: Studies That Suggest a 2%-3% Withdrawal Rate May Be a Good Starting Point

What William Bernstein has to Say

William J. Bernstein is a well-respected financial theorist who is referenced in many of the articles I've read on the safe withdrawal question. In these articles he expresses concern you could be eating dog food if you use a high withdrawal rate.

Mr. Bernstein further discusses the topic in this three-part series titled *The Retirement Calculator from Hell*. In Part 3 he comments:

> The historically naive investor (or academic) might consider reducing his monthly withdrawals to a very low level to maximize his chances of success. But history teaches us that depriving ourselves to boost our 40-year success probability much beyond 80% is a fool's errand. … But if you believe that we're about to encounter a bad returns sequence or simply wish to leave a few baubles to your heirs, you're right back to 3% again.[9]

What Wade Pfau has to Say

Wade Pfau is a vocal modern-day opponent of using a 4% withdrawal rate. Wade is a retirement researcher who has a Ph.D. in economics from Princeton and is currently a Professor of Retirement Income at The American College. He has a popular blog, appropriately called *Wade Pfau's Retirement Researcher Blog*.

A 2013 article in the *Journal of Financial Planning* by Pfau, Michael Finke, and David M. Blanchett, titled *The 4 Percent Rule Is Not Safe in a Low-Yield World*, states:

> As Pfau (2010) showed, the demonstrated success of the 4 percent rule is partly an anomaly of U.S. market returns-during the 20th century. ... This research also shows that a 2.5 percent real withdrawal rate will result in an estimated 30-year failure rate of 10 percent. Few clients will be satisfied spending such a small amount in retirement.[10]

With all due respect to Wade, I certainly hope he is wrong, because you may not have to worry about retirement as you may not ever be able to save enough to stop working.

What Michael Nairne has to Say

After reading all these academic studies, I started wondering what someone who manages money for clients in the "real world" would say. This led me to ask Michael Nairne, CFP, RFP, CFA, president of Tacita Capital Inc. who writes the *Serious Money* column for the *Financial Post*, for an opinion. I solicited Michael's opinion since we have mutual clients and I have come to appreciate that he is not only technically savvy, but a stock market historian. In a conversation, Michael suggested that the problem with the 4% rule is "that a singular historic 'backtest' represents just one perspective on withdrawal rates."

As illustrated in his article, *The Plight of the Conservative Retiree*, Michael says "the underlying average annual real return experience that funded these assumptions was about 2% for government bonds and 7% for equities. Expected annual real returns going forward are much lower today – about 1% for government bonds and 5% or so for stocks." He feels that for the typical large-cap and bond portfolio, a lower number is better – say 3% or so.[11]

Safe Withdrawal Rates – Tweaks and Variations for Today's World

Colleen M. Jaconetti and Francis M. Kinniry Jr. wrote a 2010 research report titled *A more dynamic approach to spending for investors in retirement*. The authors express some concerns about the 4% rule (constant dollar amount withdrawal adjusted for inflation).

They note that the common alternative to the 4% rule, basing your spending on a percentage of your portfolio's actual value at the end of the prior year, can also be problematic in that your withdrawal rates may fluctuate widely in the short-term, while your actual short-term costs are fixed.

Jaconetti and Kinniry attempt to address the limitations of the two above alternatives by introducing a hybrid approach to sustainable spending. They suggest you consider applying a ceiling and a floor to percentage-based withdrawals. Under this approach:

> The investor calculates each year's spending by taking a stated percentage of the prior year-end portfolio balance. The investor also calculates a 'ceiling' and 'floor' by applying chosen percentages to the prior year's spending amount. The investor then compares the three results. If the newly calculated spending amount exceeds the ceiling, the investor limits spending to the ceiling amount; if the calculated spending is below the floor, the investor increases spending to the floor amount.[12]

Todd Tresidder, a financial coach, wrote a terrific article titled *Are Safe Withdrawal Rates Really Safe?* If you are not sick of this topic yet, I strongly suggest you read his article. He says that: "Unfortunately, no simple model has surfaced to replace the 4% rule (which probably explains why it has persisted despite inaccuracy)."[13]

He then provides a four step process to serve as a guideline for a safe withdrawal rate that includes a "correct and adjust" step. Essentially he is saying stay flexible. You should feel free to adjust a 4% withdrawal rate to 3%, reduce or eliminate the inflation adjustment, or alter any part of your withdrawal strategy to protect your retirement fund.

Planning – It Is Not an Eight Letter Word

Please keep this very poignant excerpt from the Trinity Study in mind when considering your safe withdrawal rate:

> The word *planning* is emphasized because of the great uncertainties in the stock and bond markets. Mid-course corrections likely will be required, with the actual dollar amounts withdrawn adjusted downward or upward relative to the plan. The investor needs to keep in mind that selection of a withdrawal rate is not a matter of contract but rather a matter of planning.[14]

I would suggest that planning should not be limited to your withdrawal rate, but should also be considered with respect to the accumulation of your retirement nest egg.

Part 5

In Part 4 of this series, I reviewed various studies and commentaries to help you determine an appropriate safe withdrawal rate for your retirement nest egg. I also provided alternatives and variations to the safe withdrawal guidelines. In this section, I will examine the factors that can impact both the funding of your nest egg and your withdrawal rate in retirement. The unpredictable nature of most of these factors makes it virtually impossible to determine a definitive retirement number, and is why I say "heck if I know or anyone else does" as to how much money you need to retire.

Your Longevity – The Ultimate Wildcard

It goes without saying that if we knew how long we would live, retirement planning would be a lot simpler. Unfortunately, the best we can do is plan based on longevity studies and family medical history. The Vanguard paper I mentioned in Part 3 of this series references such a study by the Society of Actuaries which found "there is an 80% chance that at least one spouse will live to age 85, a 55% chance that one will live to age 90 and 25% chance one spouse will reach 95."[15]

In Canada, the average male lives to approximately age 79 and the average female lives to approximately 84. Based on the above, your retirement planning should at a minimum assume one spouse will live to at least 95 years old.

Inflation – Grasping for the Unknown

The rate of inflation can drastically alter your retirement savings and consumption. An economic environment of low market returns and high inflation can severely impact the funds you accumulate to fund your retirement and the real returns you achieve in retirement. Conversely, interest rates tend to rise with inflation, providing a potential buffer if you lock in higher interest rates and inflation subsides (I remember Canada Savings Bonds ("CSBs") paying 19.5% interest in 1981 when inflation was around 12.5%, however inflation was back down to 4.5% by the end of 1983 and many people were very pleased they had CSBs or Guaranteed Investment Certificates ("GICs") paying very high rates of interest for many years). An average inflation rate of 2% will mean that the $50,000 you expect to spend in retirement in 2014 dollars will require approximately $61,000 in spending in 2024.

One of the criticisms of the 4% rule is that the model's cumulative inflation adjustment may force you to take larger and larger withdrawals without regard to your actual spending requirements. As there have been studies that show spending tends to decrease as you age, some experts feel the model is flawed.

Sequence of Returns – Bull vs. Bear Markets Upon Your Retirement

The various studies that support a 4% retirement withdrawal included periods of both bear and bull markets. If you are lucky enough to retire at the beginning of a bull market, your retirement funding will be drastically different than if you retire at the beginning of a bear market. William Bengen, in his original 1994 article, said: "This is a powerful warning (particularly appropriate for recent retirees) not to increase their rate of withdrawal just because of a few good years early in retirement. Their 'excess returns' early may be needed to balance off weaker returns later."[16]

It is interesting to note that Mr. Bengen showed that even if you started retirement in the great depression or in the recession of 1973-1974 (which also included a period of high inflation), your money would still have lasted over 30 years, because of the power of stock market recoveries.

However, Moshe Milevsky and Anna Abaimova, in a report for MetLife, very clearly reflect the dramatic difference in retirement outcomes you will have when you have negative market returns early in your retirement vs. later in your retirement.[17]

On his blog in a post titled, *Trinity Study Updates*, Wade Pfau states that: "In fact, the wealth remaining 10 years after retirement combined with the cumulative inflation during those 10 years can explain 80 percent of the variation in a retiree's maximum sustainable withdrawal rate after 30 years."[18]

Thus, prudent planning would be to start your retirement following a bear market.

Registered vs. Non-Registered Accounts

The allocation of your retirement funds between registered (RRSPs, Locked-In Retirement Accounts ["LIRAs"], pensions, etc.) and non-registered accounts (bank, investment, Tax-Free Savings Account [TFSA], etc.) will have a significant impact upon your cash flow in retirement. If you consider all the money in those accounts as capital, the capital in the registered accounts is fully taxable, meaning that if you are a high income tax rate taxpayer, you may be paying as much as 46% or higher upon the withdrawal of those funds. For non-registered accounts, the withdrawal of capital is tax-free. This issue raises the much-debated question of TFSA vs. RRSP as you accumulate your retirement nest egg, and for those who own corporations, the issue of salary vs. dividend. The drawdown of your RRSP/RRIF (Registered Retirement Income Fund) and/or funds from your holding company in a tax-effective manner requires a detailed analysis of your specific situation and cannot be addressed here in a generic manner; however, suffice to say, it is an important cash flow issue.

Home Sweet Home

Some planners suggest you try and exclude your home from your retirement savings and have it serve as a back-up for any retirement shortfall. However, for many people, part of their retirement will include at least the incremental benefit of downsizing their home. For others, their retirement will only be funded by selling their home and moving into an apartment or reverse-mortgaging their home.

Spending in Retirement – Sharpen Your Pencil

If you are diligent about this process, you should be able to at least determine a ballpark number for your anticipated spending upon retirement. The spending wildcard for many people is travel. Good health will allow for years of travel, while poor health will not only restrict how much you can travel, but could lead to significant medical costs. In a perfect retirement model, you would factor in greater spending as you begin retirement and smaller spending as you grow older (7-10 years after retirement, many people tend to slow down and spend less either because of health issues or because their body cannot handle the hectic pace of early retirement). In addition, you need to consider occasional and lump sum expenditures.

Pensions – The Older You Are, the More You Appreciate Them

If there is one thing this series has revealed to me, it's that I truly underestimated the worth of a defined benefit pension plan. I had never really considered the possibility of purchasing an annuity in retirement; however, the more calculations I undertook, the more I realized that without a company pension plan, it may be prudent to consider purchasing at least a small annuity in my retirement to provide some comfort that I will not outlive my retirement funds.

If you have a pension plan that covers off most of your retirement spending needs, you are afforded the freedom to take greater equity risk in retirement since you can withstand stock market swings, knowing your day-to-day costs are covered off by your pension. Those without a pension face the dilemma of whether to annuitize some portion of their retirement funds or not.

Healthcare Coverage – Will We Be Fully Covered in 25 Years?

As Canadians, we assume we will always have full medical coverage. But who knows if the government will have the money in 25 years to support a top-heavy population. In addition, if your health deteriorates and you require private care, all your retirement funds could be eaten up by those costs.

Interest Rates – Will They Ever Rise?

People have been expecting interest rates to rise for several years. Many of those same people now think the US government will be forced to keep rates low for the foreseeable future. Selfishly, higher interest rates would be welcomed by many people in or near retirement. A spike in interest rates would likely cause some disgruntled stock market investors to re-allocate their equity investments to fixed income instruments.

Inheritances – No One Plans for an Inheritance, Do They?

Baby boomers will inherit a massive amount of money in the next 20 years or so. However, the size of individual inheritances will fluctuate widely based on the longevity of their parents. In Chapter 3, I discussed whether you should plan for an anticipated inheritance (*Is It Morbid or Realistic to Plan for an Inheritance?*). I suggested that if you are certain you will inherit money, you should at least consider factoring a discounted amount of your potential inheritance into your retirement planning.

Lifestyle in Retirement

For Canadians who live in large cities and have expensive homes and lifestyles, an easy solution to an underfunded retirement is to downsize/sell your home and move to a less expensive city. Whether you are willing to do that is another question.

Evolving into Retirement – Keeping the Income Stream Alive

Stan Tepner, CPA, CA, MBA, CFP, TEP, First Vice-President & investment advisor with CIBC Wood Gundy, and an advisor to some of my clients, told me in conversation he "often finds many people consider retirement an absolute event. One day you are working and the next you're golfing." He adds that "more and more people 'evolve' into retirement. They may shift into part-time employment or self-employment. This shift may be required for financial reasons or because you wish to keep your mind sharp. Either way, the extra income will assist in funding your retirement needs, especially if you have a savings shortfall because of poor market returns or you have just miscalculated your actual retirement needs."

Part 6

Parts 1-5 of this series highlighted the challenge in determining a definitive retirement number. Nevertheless, against my better judgment, you will receive some simplistic retirement nest egg calculations since we all like to know what everyone else thinks their number should be. Who the heck knows if any of these numbers will be in the ballpark or not.

Before I get to the numbers, you will read about some Canadian income tax idiosyncrasies and the impact income taxes and inflation have on your anticipated retirement withdrawal amount.

Made-In-Canada Idiosyncrasies

One significant issue for retired Canadians is that your annual minimum RRIF withdrawal starts at 7.38% and averages approximately 8% of your actual RRIF balance over the first 10 years. If your spouse is younger, you can elect to use their age to calculate your minimum RRIF withdrawal amount, which will lower your yearly required withdrawal. In either case, where the majority of your retirement funds are in your RRIF, the required withdrawal may be substantially higher than the 3%-4% you plan to withdraw annually from your retirement nest egg (however, as per my example for Mr. and Mrs. Bean below, if you can split pension income with your spouse, the income tax cost of the excess withdrawal may be mitigated).

A discussion of how to manage the drawdown of your RRSP and take into account the minimum RRIF withdrawals is too fact-specific and beyond the scope of this series.

For higher income Canadians, their OAS may be clawed back as their retirement income increases. For 2014, the clawback starts at $71,592 and your OAS is fully clawed-back at $115,715.

I Am The Blunt Bean Counter – so Let's Get Tax-Centric

As discussed way back in Part 1 of this series, the 4% withdrawal rule ignores income tax. Thus, I will provide you with some examples of how income taxes may impact your selected retirement withdrawal rate. These examples illustrate the tax-centric framework I use for one of my own retirement nest egg estimates, which I then compare with other retirement calculators, formulas, etc., proposed by other expert retirement planners.

You will note my model is just a variation on the 4% rule and still ignores investment fees. However, I am going to assume you use low-cost Exchange-Traded Funds ("ETFs") so that your costs are minimal, or if you use an investment advisor, your returns are at least market after accounting for your management fees (ha ha). I am also going to assume the yearly inflation adjustment under the 4% rule will cover off inflation, if not overcompensate for it. Just accept these assumptions for the time being. I know Michael James is flipping with the investment fee assumption.

Sample Data – Mr. and Mrs. Bean

Let's say Mr. and Mrs. Bean each expect to receive full OAS (approx. $6,500) upon retirement and that Mr. Bean and Mrs. Bean anticipate they will receive $12,000 and $6,000 respectively a year in CPP retirement benefits. Finally, assume Mr. and Mrs. Bean will have equal RRIFs or make the election to split pension income such that they will each receive $50,000 in RRIF payments in Scenario 1, $40,000 in Scenario 2, $30,000 in Scenario 3, $25,000 in Scenario 4, and $20,000 in Scenario 5.

Using the sample data above, here is the Beans' income tax situation upon their retirement:

Mr. Bean	Scenario 1	Scenario 2	Scenario 3	Scenario 4	Scenario 5
OAS	$6,500	$6,500	$6,500	$6,500	$6,500
CPP	$12,000	$12,000	$12,000	$12,000	$12,000
RRIF	$50,000	$40,000	$30,000	$25,000	$20,000
Total income	$68,500	$58,500	$48,500	$43,500	$38,500
Tax payable	$14,400	$11,100	$7,700	$5,800	$4,500
Net after-tax amount	$54,100	$47,400	$40,800	$37,700	$34,000

Mrs. Bean	Scenario 1	Scenario 2	Scenario 3	Scenario 4	Scenario 5
OAS	$6,500	$6,500	$6,500	$6,500	$6,500
CPP	$6,000	$6,000	$6,000	$6,000	$6,000
RRIF	$50,000	$40,000	$30,000	$25,000	$20,000
Total income	$62,500	$52,500	$42,500	$37,500	$32,500
Tax payable	$12,600	$9,100	$5,600	$4,200	$3,000
Net after-tax amount	$49,900	$43,400	$36,900	$33,300	$29,500
Combined after-tax	$104,000	$90,800	$77,700	$71,000	$63,500

The Tax Effect – Ouch

In Scenario 1, Mr. and Mrs. Bean will pay almost as much in personal income tax ($27,000) as they receive in OAS and CPP ($31,000). Consequently, their true cash available for spending is essentially the gross withdrawal from their RRIFs, likely a huge cash flow surprise for Mr. and Mrs. Bean. In Scenario 2, taxes eat up approximately two-thirds of Mr. and Mrs. Bean's pension income. For Scenarios 3-5, the impact of taxes, though still significant, starts to decrease as a percentage of pension income and overall income under each of those scenarios.

Playing with Numbers to Get a Tax-Centric Number

At this point, let's play with some of these numbers and see if we can come up with a crude ballpark number for the Beans' retirement nest egg. As I stated in Part 1, this framework is clearly limited, is based on the 4% withdrawal rule, has no academic basis, and should not be relied upon as the sole determinant for your own retirement planning.

Determine Your Spending Requirements

One of the most important inputs into any retirement calculation is your anticipated spending. Mr. Bean, who is an anal accountant, has used Quicken for years to track his spending and can project which of his expenses he will still have in retirement. The amount he needs to add to his projected spending amount for travel is his "retirement wildcard", but Mr. Bean is comfortable he can estimate this amount and not be materially wrong. Your spending requirement should really be a yearly calculation and should typically account for higher spending in the early years of your retirement and lower spending in the later years, plus account for one-time expenses like a car purchase, helping to pay for a child's wedding, or assisting your child in buying a house; however, for this crude calculation, I just used a set spending rate.

Reverse-Engineering Mr. Bean's Retirement Needs

[Note: For purposes of this example I am assuming all the Beans' funds come from an RRIF to exaggerate the income tax effect. In reality, you will probably have anywhere from 20-40% of your retirement funds in a non-registered account. In addition, I do not try to account for the fact that the required RRIF withdrawal may be in excess of 4%.]

Once Mr. Bean determines his spending requirements, I can work backwards to help him determine his retirement number under my tax-centric formula. For example, if I assume the Beans' spending requirement is going to be $71,000 a year in retirement and they have $31,000 in pension benefits, the Beans will need to make up a $40,000 retirement shortfall before I factor in income taxes. By coincidence, Scenario 5 reflects that exact situation. The Beans will each draw $20,000 from their RRIFs and have a combined income before tax of $71,000 ($38,500 + $32,500).

Of course, Scenario 5 reflects that after tax, they will only have $63,500 to spend, which is $7,500 short of their needs. Thus I need to gross-up the $40,000 withdrawal so the Beans can achieve their required retirement objective of $71,000 a year. Luckily I have a tax program that makes this easy to determine (you can do this with your personal tax program if you do your own taxes, or use an online calculator) and when I run the numbers, I determine the Beans will need to take $50,000 (or $25,000 each) from their RRIFs (instead of the $40,000, or $20,000 each, I required before tax in Scenario 5) to net out to their required $71,000 a year spending requirement. Again by a strange coincidence, this is essentially Scenario 4.

Since the Beans will need approximately $50,000 before inflation for each year of retirement (in addition to their CPP and OAS), I can now utilize the 4% withdrawal rule to estimate the amount of money they will need to retire. The magic number is $1,250,000 ($50,000/.04), which if you believe the 4% rule, will allow the Beans to withdraw $50,000 plus inflation for approximately 30 years, or $71,000 after-tax including their pension income. If the Beans want to provide a measure of safety and use a 3% withdrawal rate, they would require a nest egg of $1,666,667 ($50,000/.03). Mr. Bean, however, told me to stick with the 4%, since as an accountant, he has led a stressed life and does not anticipate making it past 85 anyway.

The above calculation results in an inflated magic number, as it assumes 100% in registered funds. In reality, the number would be based on a drawdown between your registered and non-registered accounts.

When I told Mr. Bean these results, he was thoroughly depressed. However, with my warped sense of humour, I went on to tell him that if he were to retire in 10 years and he required $50,000 in non-indexed RRIF withdrawals (CPP and OAS are indexed for inflation), he would actually require approximately $61,000 in yearly withdrawals if inflation averaged 2%. That would push him closer to Scenario 2 above. That would mean he would require almost $80,000 in RRIF payments, and using a 4% withdrawal rate he would need to have $2,000,000 at retirement, a staggering number. Personally, I think you cannot look at a 2% inflation rate and just inflate your spending expectation. I would suggest wage increases may partially offset these increases and presumably the extra 10 years of investment returns and new deposits would make it possible to get to $2M in 10 years even if they don't have $1.25M now. In any event, it is a sobering calculation.

Comparing Apples to Oranges to Pineapples

When I started this series, I was foolish enough to think that I could utilize the Beans' income and spending parameters to provide you with comparable nest egg numbers using various retirement experts' formulas. However, as I discussed in Part 5, there are multiple variables and assumptions that affect each calculation, which makes an apples to apples comparison impossible. This will be vividly demonstrated as I walk through the various comparisons below.

Yet, I thought it would still be interesting to see how various retirement experts and their formulas, equations, etc. compare when given the same retirement spending level and the same pension numbers. It is enlightening, if not slightly amusing, to see how the retirement variables are applied and the significant variances in the final nest egg determination.

What a Financial Planner Says

I figured I should include some state of the art financial planning software for this exercise and thus, I asked a financial planner I work with to run some numbers on his software for me based on the $50,000 RRIF requirement and $31,000 of pension income. In the end our comparison was not apples to apples. His software forced him to make various assumptions I could not include in my crude calculation, and he wanted to use a 3.5% real rate of return. He also decided he wanted to allocate the non-registered and registered accounts equally, amongst other assumptions I could not make with my limited tax-centric model. So what did his software reflect as the required nest egg? His number was $1,335,000.

Jim Otar's Retirement Asset Multiplier

I next turned to Jim Otar, a financial planner and mechanical engineer (what is with engineers and retirement?). Jim is the author of *Unveiling the Retirement Myth*. He considers there to be three basic risks for retirement financing:

1. Longevity risk

2. Market risk

3. Inflation risk

He uses an asset multiplier to factor in these risks. Jim does an awesome job of explaining these using "plain English" in his article *Do we have enough to retire?*[19]

When I use Jim's multiplier of 28 x my $40,000 pre-tax shortfall, I come to required retirement assets of $1,120,000.

Michael James

I asked Michael to use his calculator that I discussed in Part 3 to determine the Beans' required nest egg. He assumed an allocation of 15% in bonds, 15% fully safe, and 70% in stocks. He also assumed a 4% real return for stocks and a 2% real return for the bonds. He also assumed a very efficient ETF portfolio with fees of only 0.2%.

Michael determined if the Beans want to live indefinitely, they will need a nest egg of approximately $1,680,000. If they plan to live to the age of 95, they will need approximately $1,070,000. If they plan to live to 90, they will need around $960,000 or so.

If Michael used a 2% Management Expense Ratio ("MER") instead of his ultra low cost MER of 0.2%, his figures jump to $3,250,000 if you plan to live indefinitely, $1,270,000 for age 95 and, $1,090,000 for age 90.

Summary of $71,000 Spending Requirement

If the Beans require $71,000 to spend in retirement after tax (including $31,000 in pension income), the various calculations would suggest that they should be shooting for a nest egg of $1,100,000 at the low end to $1,350,000 at the high end.

As noted above, I have taken liberties with some of the calculations and the variables would change for your specific assumptions and facts. Like I say in my title, who the heck really knows what you need to retire; all these numbers may be consistently wrong, but the above at least provides a starting point of some sort, even if it's simplistic.

What If the Beans Have a $104,000 after-Tax Spending Requirement?

Since my chart for the Beans includes a scenario (#1) where they have a requirement for $104,000 in after-tax spending ($131,000 in pre-tax income), let's see what the various formulas would reflect as their nest egg requirement for that level of spending.

Blunt Bean Counter – **$2,500,000** ($100,000 RRIF/.04% =$2,500,000 for a 100% registered account).

Jim Otar – **$2,044,000** (as the $104,000 is an after-tax spending amount and Jim uses a pre-tax spending shortfall, I have estimated that spending shortfall to be approximately $73,000).

Financial Planner – **$2,250,000** using the same variables as noted in the prior example.

Michael James – If you want to live indefinitely you will need approximately $3,370,000; if you live to age 95 the magic number drops to around **$2,150,000**; at 90, it's **$1,920,000**; and finally, at 85 it's approximately **$1,650,000**.

If Michael used a 2% MER instead of his ultra low cost MER of 0.2%, his figures jump to $6,510,0000 if you plan to live indefinitely, $2,530,000 for age 95, and $2,190,000 for age 90.

Summary of $104,000 Spending Requirement

If the Beans require $104,000 to spend in retirement after tax (including $31,000 in pension income), the various calculations would suggest that they should be shooting for a nest egg of $2,000,000 at the low end to $2,500,000 at the high end.

Canadians Know Best

A recent BMO Harris Private Banking survey said that Canadians with investable assets of $1 million or more say they need on average $2.3 million to live out their ideal retirement lifestyle.[20] Based on the above, it looks like they are in the ballpark.

Final Caveat

Throughout this series, I've shared with you my research and analysis and provided you with as much information as possible so that you can try and determine (or at least consider) the assets you need to accumulate for your own retirement nest egg. There is not one definitive number. Keep in mind, one size does not fit all. My retirement funding includes the sale of my partnership interest; yours may include the sale of a business or a severance payment for taking early retirement. The point being, we all have unique situations.

Conclusion – This Series Is Finally Over!!

After going through the analysis I provided to you, I've determined that I am much further away from my retirement goal than I had anticipated and I will still be working for several more years. I now wish I had a company pension. The largest surprise of this exercise to me was that I may give consideration to purchasing an annuity with some portion of my retirement funds to ensure I have a constant minimum cash flow. Depressing as this exercise was, it brought some clarity to my retirement planning. I also realized that I have no idea whose Monte Carlo simulator will hit the jackpot, and that historical data can be interpreted in so many ways that it leaves your head spinning.

I do know a multitude of factors beyond my control may impact my expected withdrawal rate (see Part 5 for the laundry list), and thus as a result I will have to:

1. Be flexible in my spending requirements and may need to be open to working part-time in retirement.

2. Review, revise, and refine my retirement plan on a consistent basis to account for financial and life events and any changes in my behaviour.

In conclusion, I hope my quest or journey for freedom ~~55, 65,~~ 75, helps guide your retirement planning.

---

1 Bengen, William P. "Determining Withdrawal Rates Using Historical Data." *Journal of Financial Planning* 7, no. 4 (1994): 171-180.

2 Bengen, William P. *Conserving Client Portfolios during Retirement*. Denver: FPA Press, 2006.

3 Bengen, Bill. "How Much Is Enough?" *Financial Advisor*, May 1, 2012.

4 Bengen, William P. "Determining Withdrawal Rates Using Historical Data." *Journal of Financial Planning* 7, no. 4 (1994): 171-172.

5 Cooley, Philip L., Carl M Hubbard, and Daniel T Walz. "Retirement Savings: Choosing a Withdrawal Rate That Is Sustainable." *AAII Journal* 20, 3 (1998): 16–21.

6 Williams, Rob. "Is the 4% Rule Still Appropriate?" The Schwab Center for Financial Research. June 4, 2013.

7 Bruno, Maria A, Colleen M Jaconetti, and Yan Zilbering. "Revisiting the '4% Spending Rule'." The Vanguard Group. August, 2012: 2.

8 Ibid., 3.

9 Bernstein, William J. "The Retirement Calculator from Hell, Part III: Eat, Drink, and Be Merry." EfficientFrontier.com.

10 Finke, Michael, Wade D Pfau, and David M Blanchett. "The 4 Percent Rule Is Not Safe in a Low-Yield World." *Journal of Financial Planning* 26, 6 (2013): 54.

11 Nairne, Michael. "The Plight of the Conservative Retiree." Tacita Capital. June 30, 2012.

12 Jaconetti, Colleen M, and Francis M Kinniry Jr. "A more dynamic approach to spending for investors in retirement." The Vanguard Group. November, 2010: 4.

13 Tressider, Todd R. "Are Safe Withdrawal Rates Really Safe?" *Journal of Personal Finance* 11, n 1 (2012): 137.

14 Cooley, Philip L., Carl M Hubbard, and Daniel T Walz. "Retirement Savings: Choosing a Withdrawal Rate That Is Sustainable." *AAII Journal* 20, 3 (1998): 16.

15 Bruno, Maria A, Colleen M Jaconetti, and Yan Zilbering. "Revisiting the '4% Spending Rule'." The Vanguard Group. August, 2012: 5.

16 Bengen, William P. "Determining Withdrawal Rates Using Historical Data." *Journal of Financial Planning* 7, 4 (1994): 173.

17 Milevsky, Moshe A, and Anna Abaimova. "Retirement Income: The Role of Product Allocation in Sustaining Retirement Income." Metlife. White Papers, 4.

18 Phau, Wade. "Trinity Study Updates." Wade Pfau's Retirement Researcher Blog. April 1, 2011. 3c.

19 Otar, Jim. "Do We Have Enough to Retire?" Financial Post. January 25, 2012.

20 BMO Harris Private Banking. "Affluent Canadians Report They Need an Average of $2.3 Million to Retire". BMO Financial Group. BMO Harris Private Banking Study Press Release (Conducted by Pollara, March 28-April 11, 2013), January 17, 2014.

Chapter 10

Estate Freezes - A Cool Way to Tax Plan

Estate Freeze – A Tax Solution for the Succession of a Small Business

Winston Churchill once said, "Let our advance worrying become advance thinking and planning." Small business owners often worry about their exit strategy and/or succession plan. They may also be concerned about what would happen to their business if they had a health scare or received an ultimatum from a child working in their business. Often a small business owner's worry becomes their anxiety, instead of their advance planning.

As a small business owner, at the end of the day there are essentially only two exit strategy/succession options you need to plan for and/or consider:

1. A sale of your business, typically to a competitor, sometimes to current management, or (very infrequently) an actual sale to a child or other family member.

2. A transfer of the business to your children without a sale (for purpose of this discussion, I will refer to this option as an "estate freeze").

Below, I discuss how an estate freeze allows you to transfer your business tax-free to a successor (typically your children, sometimes to existing management) while continuing to control and receive remuneration from your business.

In the next article in this chapter, I will discuss Tom Deans' thoughts on this matter. Tom, who is the author of *Every Family's Business* (the best-selling family business book of all-time), believes a business should in most cases be sold and never handed over to the next generation (such as done with an estate freeze) without the parent(s) adequately being compensated for the business.[1]

What Is an Estate Freeze?

The most tax-efficient manner to transfer your business to your children is to undertake an estate freeze. An estate freeze allows your children to carry on your business, while at the same time you receive shares worth the current value of your business. In addition, once your share value is locked in, your future income tax liability with respect to your company's shares is fixed and can only decrease. Keep in mind that when you freeze the value of your company you are not receiving any monies for your shares at that time. There may be ways to monetize that value in the future, but in an estate freeze, you typically only receive shares of value, not cash.

The key risk in any estate freeze is that your children may partially or fully devalue these shares and your company. So while an estate freeze may be the most tax-efficient way to transfer your business, it may not be the best decision from an economic or monetization perspective.

In a typical estate freeze, you exchange your common shares of your corporation on a tax-free basis for preferred shares that have a permanent value ("frozen value") equal to the common shares' fair market value ("FMV") at the time of the freeze. Subsequently, a successor or successors, say your children or family trust, can subscribe for new common shares of the corporation for a nominal amount.

This concept is best explained with an example. Assume Mr. A has an incorporated business worth $3,000,000 and wants to undertake an estate freeze. In the course of the freeze, Mr. A is issued new preferred shares worth $3,000,000 and his children or a family trust subscribes for new common shares for nominal consideration. Mr. A's tax liability in relation to these shares on death, is now fixed at approximately $750,000 in Ontario. Often, a key aspect of an estate freeze is a plan to reduce the tax liability by redeeming the preferred shares on a year by year basis as discussed below.

If you have access to your lifetime capital gains exemption (currently at $800,000 but indexed beginning in 2015 for inflation), your income tax liability may be reduced when the shares are eventually sold or upon your death if you still own them at that time. Finally, you may choose to crystallize your exemption when you freeze the shares.

The preferred shares received on the freeze can be created such that they allow you to maintain voting control of your corporation until you are satisfied your children are running the company in the manner you desire. This maybe a double-edged sword, as you may tend to hold on to control long after your successors have proven themselves. This may become a contentious issue.

Preferred shares can also serve as a source of retirement income. Typically what is done is that your preferred shares are redeemed gradually. So, for example, if you need $100,000 before tax per year to live, you can redeem $100,000 of your preferred shares each year. Let's say you live 20 years and redeem a $100,000 a year. By the time of your death, you will have redeemed $2,000,000 ($100,000 x 20 years) of your preferred shares and they will now only be worth $1,000,000 ($3,000,000 original value less $2,000,000) at your death. Your income tax liability on these shares at the time of your death will now only be approximately $250,000.

The Benefits of an Estate Freeze

1. On death (something we should all be planning for), an individual is subject to a deemed disposition (i.e. a sale) on all of their assets at FMV, which would include their shares of the business. An estate freeze sets your maximum income tax liability upon this deemed sale and, as discussed above,

this liability can be lowered over the years by redeeming the shares.

2. Family members will be able to become shareholders of the business at a minimal cost and be motivated to build the business (although Tom Deans would dispute this assertion).

3. Instead of having children directly subscribe for new common shares, you can create a discretionary family trust to hold the common shares. Every year, the corporation can pay dividends to the family trust which can then allocate the dividends to family members with lower marginal tax rates. This mechanism allows for great income splitting opportunities.

4. On the eventual sale of the business, the children or family trust may realize a significant capital gain. Assuming that the business qualifies for the capital gains exemption, the family trust can allocate this capital gain to each beneficiary who may be able to use their own lifetime capital gains exemption limit to shield $800,000 or more of capital gains from income tax.

One of the more critical aspects of an estate freeze is the determination of the FMV of your business. In order to ensure that an estate freeze proceeds as smoothly as possible, the FMV of the company must be calculated. In the event that the FMV determined is challenged by the Canada Revenue Agency ("CRA"), the attributes of the preferred shares will have a purchase price adjustment clause that will let the freezer reset the FMV. The CRA has stated in the past that they will generally accept the use of a purchase price adjustment clause if a "reasonable attempt" has been made in valuing the company. Engaging a third-party independent Chartered Business Valuator to prepare a valuation report is generally accepted as a "reasonable attempt" in estimating the FMV.[2]

Issues to Consider before Implementing an Estate Freeze

An estate freeze does not make sense for all business owners. While the above benefits do sound very enticing, it depends on each owner's personal circumstances. Issues to be considered include:

1. Are you relying on the value of the company to fund your retirement? If so, it may be best to sell and ensure you have a secure retirement.

2. Do you have an identified successor (e.g. a child) able and willing to work in your business?

3. Can you bring one child into the business without creating a dispute amongst your children?

4. Are your children married, and how may a divorce or separation impact the business?

Personally, I am a proponent of family discussions and getting over the money taboo. I cannot overstate the importance of having a detailed discussion with your family if you plan to hand your business over to one or more of your children. If you pass that hurdle, you must speak with your accountant and lawyer to ensure you understand the implications of the freeze and how to properly implement the corporate restructuring. Finally, your tax advisor will want to structure the freeze such that it can be "thawed" if the business suffers a setback due to the economy, or your children prove incapable of running the company.

Are Estate Freezes the Wrong Solution for Family Business Succession? – Part 1

I discussed how an estate freeze provides an efficient income tax solution for the succession of your family business by allowing you to lock in the value of your business and pass the ownership tax-free to your children. However, a freeze does not provide you with immediate liquidity, nor does it require your children to risk their own capital. Some family succession experts believe an estate freeze is a misplaced income tax solution, when what is really required is a business solution.

I was one of the "experts" on a panel that discussed family succession. The guest speaker and main attraction for the night was Tom Deans (yes, believe it or not, I was not the draw). Tom is the author of *Every Family's Business: 12 Common Sense Questions to Protect Your Wealth*, the best-selling family business book of all-time with more than 500,000 copies sold. Tom is an outspoken advocate of parents taking care of themselves, which often means selling their business (whether to a competitor, their own child, or management), rather than just handing it over to their children for free (via an estate freeze).

Tom's suggestion to monetize your business, rather than to hand it over to your children, runs counter to the commonly-held belief that your business is your legacy and that the ultimate family business is multigenerational. For many business owners, I would suggest that Tom's advice to sell and safeguard your retirement is often the prudent decision.

Tom says an "estate freeze usually sets the stage for what I like to describe as the beginning of the 'perpetuity project'. This is when a family shifts its thinking away from the business as a money-making asset and toward the business as a legacy, with the goal of 'longevity' trumping all other strategic options for creating value."[3]

With statistics suggesting that only 30% of family businesses transition successfully to the second generation and a meager 10% to a third generation[4], Tom may be correct that many parents are compliant in destroying their business by trying to ensure its perpetuity.

Why Parents May Choose to Undertake an Estate Freeze

In my experience, parents often cite three reasons for preferring an estate freeze over an outright sale to an arm's-length party or to one of their children:

1. They see the family business as an annuity, so why sell for $4,000,000 ($3,200,000 or so after tax) when it will make $4,000,000 every four to five years indefinitely if the business continues as it is or grows.

2. They feel they can easily redeem enough of their frozen shares each year to cover their living expenses, so why burden the children with additional debt?

3. What is the point in selling shares to their children if their children need to borrow from the bank to purchase the shares, especially since if the business goes sour, the parents figure they may need to step up and cover the default anyways?

What Is so Bad About an Estate Freeze?

As many accountants can attest to, often a well-intentioned estate freeze that has saved the family thousands or even hundreds of thousands of dollars in tax ends up being the catalyst to family conflict and/or the ruin of the family's business. Here are some of the downsides to an estate freeze:

1. In undertaking a freeze, shares are issued for no consideration. The children have no risk capital invested in the company, which can alter their commitment to the business.

2. Whether a company's share value increases due to market forces or because of the children's efforts or non-efforts is irrelevant; your children may end up making far more than you ever did, despite you handing them a turnkey operation (and that may be fine with you).

3. An estate freeze requires decisions regarding which child(ren) will work in the business, how they will be compensated, and which of them get shares and what percentage of the shares. All these decisions can blow up. For example, let's say you undertake an estate freeze and give your daughter who will work in the business all the shares of the business (which are in theory worthless at the date of the freeze, since you have all the current value in your special shares; say your shares are worth $2,000,000 in this example). You leave your other two children say $100,000 each in your will to "compensate" them for not being involved in the freeze. Imagine the sibling conflict if the business grows to $3,000,000 in value. The child working in the business has benefited to the tune of one million dollars ($3,000,000-$2,000,000 freeze value) plus a full-time job, compared to the $100k the other children will receive in the will.

4. Parents often like the concept of freezes because it locks in the maximum amount of income tax they will owe on death, however, the freeze is also often viewed as a way for them to slow down and move away from the business. If the child who takes over the business makes a mess of the family company,

mom or dad or both are often forced to step back in to save the company – not exactly the stress-free retirement they imagined.

5. In a blog post by Tom, he states that an estate freeze "magnifies family genius – and incompetence – precisely because the market rules of ownership were violated through gifting, all in the name of saving tax. Families pay the highest price when they lose their mutual trust and respect for one another when gifting goes bad. And when trust is lost, family members resorting to litigation is the saddest progression of a family business in decline."[5]

The Benefits of an Estate Freezes

My personal experience with estate freezes has been good. While the overwhelming majority of my clients over the years have sold their businesses, there have been several that have frozen their companies and everything worked out. I would say that is because most of these clients were able to distinguish which child(ren) deserved to work in the business and were committed to the business (in most cases, the children have been uniformly intelligent and often academically brighter than their parents, though not necessarily as street smart). The parents also gave significant thought to how they would compensate the children both involved in the business and those excluded from involvement. Finally, and probably the most important, the parents tried to understand the sibling dynamic within their families and whether a freeze made sense within these family dynamics.

When I spoke to Tom about this before his speech, he asked me: "If all these children were so committed to the business and so bright, why would they not have agreed to purchase shares from their parents?"

Now you may be thinking to yourself that an estate freeze may not be the succession-planning panacea it is marketed as, at least from the non-tax perspective. In Part 2, I will discuss the issues Tom considers vital in regard to selling or transitioning your family business.

Are Estate Freezes the Wrong Solution for Family Business Succession? – Part 2

In Part 1, I discussed why an estate freeze may not be the right solution for a family's business succession plan and why Tom Deans considers an estate freeze to generally be the absolute wrong way to go about transferring a family business.

Next, I will discuss my interpretation of Tom's thoughts based on a panel discussion I participated in with him, my reading of his book, and a review of interviews he has given. To be absolutely clear, these are my interpretations and Tom has not reviewed or commented in any way.

Buy the Business, Are You Kidding Me?

In the postscript to Tom's book, *Every Family's Business: 12 Common Sense Questions to Protect Your Wealth*, he says the one part of his presentation that always elicits an uneasy response is when he says "in this room there are children who believe their parents will gift their business to them and parents who believe their children will purchase their business." He goes on to say "this lack of clarity over the future ownership of the business is the greatest source of conflict and wealth destruction in a business."[6]

What Tom is poignantly noting is the lack of communication between parents and their children and the unspoken assumptions that are often far from the truth. A parent needs to be honest with their children if their expectation is that their children will have to purchase the family business. Children need to be honest with their parents about whether or not they are willing to purchase shares in the business or if they even have an interest in carrying on the business. The best business families are able to talk openly, honestly and frankly about money, business, and family succession.

161

Just Sell the Damn Thing

Tom says "The legacy is not the business. The legacy is the family." Many business owners believe their greatest legacy is their company and their job as entrepreneurs is to transition that business into their children's hands. Tom suggests that owners need to grant themselves permission to take care of themselves first by selling for cash and looking at their business as an instrument of wealth creation. Although the business will typically be sold to competitors, Tom has no problem offering the business to children, as long as they purchase it on commercial terms and take on the risk of ownership (children may get preferential payment terms).

Tom says that when children find out they will not be gifted the business (through an estate freeze) they are often perturbed, however, when it is explained to them that someone is paying mom or dad millions of dollars, some of which may be allocated to them immediately or will ensure a significant inheritance for them in the future, they suddenly change their tune. Essentially, Tom is saying that the equity in your business does not have to be passed down as shares in the business, but can be passed as liquid wealth to your children down the road. To deal with the liquid wealth created by a sale, Tom wrote a second book entitled *Willing Wisdom: 7 Questions Successful Families Ask*.[7]

Transitioning Your Business to Your 65-Year-Old Child

If a parent decides against selling the business and undertakes an estate freeze, often the parent becomes their own worst enemy. Tom half-jokingly noted during our panel discussion that when your parent has a heart attack at 71, 20 years ago they died. Now doctors put in a coronary stent and your parent is good for another 20 years. So when parents tell a child "it will all be yours one day", that "one day" could be when you turn 65, and up until you obtain control of the company, your parents may keep their thumbs on you (since they often maintain voting control). Parents, skipping a generation is not succession planning!

Find the End before It Finds You

Tom says that in many cases, your succession plan as an owner is no plan, and until you suffer a health event, you have no urgency to plan. He suggests that it is important to start planning from day one, while you are healthy and clear of mind. Determine if there is a buyer in the house (family member) and as noted above, do not assume your children will be the buyer. He feels that if your children will not put up their own money (or obtain their own bank financing) to buy some or all of your shares, you should look elsewhere. If a child is not willing to risk their own capital, Tom feels that means they are either not committed to the business or they truly feel the business is old and past its freshness date.

Whether you want your business to be enticing to your children or to an arm's-length buyer, you must ensure your business adapts to changes and risks in the marketplace and that you continuously strive to improve operations and efficiency. By doing such, you make your company more valuable to an outside party and more attractive for a child to risk their own capital and carry on the business.

If you own a business, I strongly suggest you read Tom's book. In the end, he boils family succession planning down to 12 common sense questions that start the family succession conversation but also cleverly have the ability to end the conversation quickly. I hope this discussion on estate freezes has given you plenty of food for thought.

---

1 Deans, Thomas William. *Every Family's Business: 12 Common Sense Questions to Protect Your Wealth*. 2nd ed. Orangeville: Détente, 2009.

2 Canada Revenue Agency. "S4-F3-C1: Price Adjustment Clauses." Canada Revenue Agency. Income Tax Folio S4-F3-C1, 2014, s 1.5.

3 Deans, Thomas. "Estate Brain Freeze: Why Saving Tax Is the Wrong Place to Start a Family Business Succession Plan." Every Family's Business Blog. April 27, 2011.

4 Deans, *Every Family's Business*, preface.

5 Deans, "Estate Brain Freeze," 2011.

6 Deans, *Every Family's Business*, 131.

7 Deans, Thomas William. *Willing Wisdom: 7 Questions Successful Families Ask*. 2nd ed. Orangeville: Détente, 2014.

Chapter 11

The Family Cottage - How to Deal With It

Transferring the Family Cottage

This is a three-part series on transferring the family cottage. The first part will deal with the historical nature of the income tax rules, while the second part will deal with the income tax implications of transferring or gifting a cottage, and finally in the third part, I will discuss alternative income tax planning opportunities that may mitigate or defer income tax upon the transfer of a family cottage.

Part 1 – There Is No Panacea

Canadians love their cottages. They are willing to put up with three-hour drives, traffic jams, never-ending repairs and maintenance, and constant hosting duties for their piece of tranquility by the lake. However, I would suggest the family cottage is one of the most problematic assets for income tax planning purposes, let alone the inherent family politics that are sure to arise.

For purposes of this discussion, I will just assume away the family politics issue. I will assume the children will each grab a beer, sit down at a table, and work out a cottage-sharing schedule to everyone's satisfaction; and while they are at it, agree on how they will share the future ownership of the cottage when their parents transfer the cottage or pass away. I would say this is a very realistic situation in Canada, not!!!

Let's also dismiss any illusions some may harbour that they can plan around the taxation issues related to cottages (or even avoid them entirely). I can tell you outright that there is no magical solution to solving the income tax issues in regard to a family cottage, just ways to mitigate or defer the issues. Many cottages were purchased years ago and have large unrealized capital gains.

So let's start by taking a step back in time. Up until 1981, each spouse could designate their own principal residence ("PR") which, in most cases, made the income tax implications of disposing or gifting a family cottage a null and void issue. The "principal residence exemption" ("PRE") in the *Income Tax Act* essentially eliminated any capital gain realized when a personal use property was sold or transferred. Families that had a home in the city and a cottage in the country typically did not have to pay tax on any capital gains realized on either property when sold or gifted.

However, for any year after 1981, a family unit (generally considered to be the taxpayer, his or his spouse or common-law partner, and unmarried minor children) can only designate one property between them for purposes of the PRE. Although the designation of a property as a PR is a yearly designation, it is only made when there is an actual disposition of a home. For example, if you owned and lived in both a cottage and a house between 2001 and 2011 and sold them both in 2011, you could choose to designate your cottage as your PR for 2001 to 2003 and your house from 2004 to 2011, or any other permutation plus one year (the Canada Revenue Agency ["CRA"] provides a bonus year because they are just a giving agency).[1]

In order to decide which property to designate for each year after 1981, it is always necessary to determine whether there is a larger gain per year on your cottage or your home in the city. Once that determination is made, in most cases it makes sense to designate the property with the larger gain per year as your personal residence for purposes of the PRE.

Part 2 – Tax Issues

As discussed above, you can only designate one property as a principal residence per family after 1981. In order to explore the income tax implications associated with transferring ownership of a cottage, I will assume both a city residence and a cottage have been purchased subsequent to 1981, and I will assume that the PRE has been fully allocated to your city home and the cottage will be the taxable property.

Many parents want to transfer their cottage to their children while they are alive, however any gift or sale to their children will result in a deemed capital gain equal to the fair market value ("FMV") of the cottage, less the original cost of the cottage, plus any renovations to the cottage. Consequently, a transfer while the owner-parent(s) is/are alive will create an income tax liability where there is an unrealized capital gain.

Alternatively, where a cottage is not transferred during one parent's lifetime and the cottage is left to the surviving spouse or common-law partner, there are no income tax issues until the death of the surviving spouse/partner. However, upon the death of the surviving spouse/partner, there will be a deemed capital gain, calculated exactly as noted above. This deemed capital gain must be reported on the terminal (final) tax return of the deceased spouse/partner.

Whether a gift or transfer of the cottage is made during your lifetime, or the property transfers to your children through your will, you will have the same income tax issue: a deemed disposition with a capital gain equal to the FMV of the cottage, less its cost.

It is my understanding that all provinces (with the exception of Alberta, Saskatchewan, and parts of rural Nova Scotia) have land transfer taxes that would be applicable on any type of cottage transfer. You should confirm whether land transfer tax is applicable in your province with your real estate lawyer

So, are there any strategies to mitigate or alleviate the income tax issue noted above? In my opinion, other than buying life insurance to cover the income tax liability, most strategies are essentially ineffective tax-wise as they only defer or partially mitigate the income tax issue. In Part 3 of this series I will summarize the income tax planning options available to transfer the family cottage.

Part 3 – Ways to Reduce the Tax Hit from the Family Cottage

The following alternatives may be available to mitigate and defer the income taxes that may arise on the transfer of a family cottage.

Life Insurance

Life insurance may prevent a forced sale of a family cottage where there is a large income tax liability upon the death of a parent, and the estate does not have sufficient liquid assets to cover the income tax liability. The downside to insurance is the cost over the years, which can be substantial. The cost of insurance over decades of potentially increasing premiums, all the while ensuring the insurance policy is large enough to cover the income tax liability, is problematic. (Alternatively one can wait until later in life to insure and take a chance on whether they can still obtain insurance.) I would suggest very few people imagined the quantum of the capital gains they would have on their cottages when they initially purchased them, so guessing at the adequate quantum of life insurance required is difficult at best. Purchasing a large last-to-die insurance policy may do the trick; however, the ultimate insurance cost over time has to be balanced against taking those funds and investing them to cover off the future income tax liability.

Gift or Sale to Your Children

As discussed in Part 2, this option is challenging as it will create a deemed capital gain, and will result in an immediate income tax liability in the year of transfer if there is an inherent capital gain on the cottage. The upside to this strategy is that if the gift or sale is undertaken at a time when there is only a small unrealized capital gain and the cottage increases in value after the transfer, most of the income tax liability is passed on to the second generation. This strategy does not eliminate the income tax issue; rather it defers it, which in turn can create even a larger income tax liability for the next generation.

If you decide to sell the cottage to your children, be advised the *Income Tax Act* provides for a five-year capital gains reserve, and thus consideration should be given to having the terms of repayment spread out over at least five years.

Transfer to a Trust

A transfer of a cottage to a trust generally results in a deemed capital gain at the time of transfer. An insidious feature of a family trust is that while the trust may be able to claim the PRE, in doing so, it can effectively preclude the beneficiaries (typically the children) of the trust from claiming the PRE on their own city homes for the period the trust designates the cottage as a principal residence.

If a parent is 65 years old or older, transferring the cottage to an Alter Ego Trust or a Joint Partner Trust is another alternative. These trusts are more effective than a standard trust, since there is no deemed disposition and no capital gain is created on the transfer. The downside is that upon the death of the parent, the cottage is deemed to be sold and any capital gain is taxed at the highest personal income tax rate, which could result in even more income tax owing.

The use of a trust can be an effective means of sheltering the cottage from probate taxes. Caution is advised if you are considering a non-Alter Ego or Joint Partner Trust, as on the 21-year anniversary date of the creation of the trust, the cottage must either be transferred to a beneficiary (should be tax-free), or the trust must pay income taxes on the property's accrued gain.

Transfer to a Corporation

A cottage can be transferred to a corporation on a tax-free basis using the rollover provisions of the *Income Tax Act*. This would avoid the deemed capital gain issue upon transfer. However, subsequent to the transfer the parents would own shares in the corporation that would result in a deemed disposition (and most likely a capital gain) upon the death of the last surviving parent. An "estate freeze" can be undertaken concurrently, which would fix the parent's income tax liability at death and allow future growth to accrue to the children; however, that is a topic for another time.

In addition, holding a cottage in a corporation may result in a taxable benefit for personal use and will eliminate any chance of claiming the PRE on the cottage for the parent and children in the future.

In summary, where there is a large unrealized capital gain on a family cottage, there will be no income tax panacea. However, one of the alternatives noted above may assist in mitigating the income tax issue and allow for the orderly transfer of the property.

I strongly encourage you to seek professional advice when dealing with this issue. There are numerous pitfalls and issues as noted above, and the advice above is general in nature and should not be relied upon for specific circumstances.

Cottages – Cost Base Additions, Are They a New CRA Audit Target?

Canadians have a love affair with their cottages. They enjoy the fresh air, the tranquility, the loons calling out, drinks on the dock, the gathering of friends and family, and in many cases they often enjoy a substantial financial profit on their cottage properties.

When a cottage property has increased in value, it often brings unwanted income tax and estate planning issues. I wrote about some of these issues earlier in this chapter.

In this article I want to discuss the fact that the CRA seems to be looking at cottage sales as audit targets, and in particular, they are reviewing additions to the original adjusted cost base ("ACB") of the cottage.

Income Tax Issues

As discussed earlier in this chapter, prior to 1982, a taxpayer and their spouse could each designate their own PR and each could claim their own PRE. Therefore, where a family owned a cottage and a family home, each spouse could potentially claim their own PRE: one on the cottage and one on the family home, and accordingly the sale of both properties would be tax-free.

Alas, the taxman felt this treatment was too generous and changed the *Income Tax Act*. Beginning in 1982, a family unit (a family unit of the taxpayer includes the taxpayer's spouse or common-law partner and unmarried children that are under 18 years old) could only designate one principal residence between them for each tax year after 1981.

As if the above is not complex enough, anyone selling a cottage must also consider the following ACB adjustments:

1. If your cottage was purchased prior to 1972, you will need to know the FMV on December 31, 1971; the FMV of your cottage on this date became your cost base when the CRA brought in capital gains taxation.

2. In 1994, the CRA eliminated the $100,000 capital gains exemption; however, they allowed taxpayers to elect to bump the ACB of properties such as real estate to their FMV to a maximum of $100,000 (subject to some restrictions not worth discussing here). Many Canadians took advantage of this election and increased the ACB of their cottages.

3. Many people have inherited cottages. When someone passes away, they are deemed to dispose of their capital property at the FMV on the date of their death (unless the property is transferred to their spouse). The person inheriting the property assumes the deceased's FMV on their death as their ACB.

The Principal Residence Exemption

As noted above, if you owned a cottage prior to 1982, you can make a PRE claim for those years on your cottage. Where the per year gain on your cottage is in excess of the per year gain on your home, you may want to consider whether for the years after 1982, it makes sense to allocate the PRE to your cottage instead of your home (if you have not already used the PRE on prior home or cottage sales). In these cases, I would suggest professional advice due to the complexity of the rules. In completing the PR designation tax form (*T2091*), there are cases where you may need the ACB and FMV at December 31, 1981, but I will ignore this issue for purposes of this discussion.

Putting Together the Pieces of the ACB Puzzle

So how do all these rules come together in determining your ACB? First, if you owned your cottage prior to 1972, you will need to determine the FMV at December 31, 1971, as that is your opening ACB. If you purchased the cottage after 1971, but before 1994, your ACB will be your purchase cost plus legal and land transfer costs. Next, you will have to determine whether you increased your ACB by electing to bump your ACB in 1994.

If you inherited the property, you will need to find out the FMV of the cottage on the date of the death of the person you inherited the property from. If the property was inherited before 1994, you will have to determine whether you increased your ACB by electing in 1994.

Finally, most people have made various capital improvements to their cottages over the years. For income tax purposes, these improvements are added to the ACB you have determined above. Examples of capital improvements would be the addition of a deck, a dock, a new roof or new windows that were better than the original roof or windows, or new well or pump. General repairs are not capital improvements, and you cannot value your own work if you are the handyman type. I would argue, however, that the cost of materials for a capital improvement would qualify if you do the work yourself.

Unfortunately, many people do not keep track of these improvements, nor do they keep their receipts (in addition, I suspect one or two cottage owners may have done the occasional cash deal with various contractors for which there will not be a supporting invoice), which brings us to the CRA, who appears to be auditing the sale of cottages more intently.

The Audit Issue

On to the audit issue (or more properly called an information request). Some accountants think the CRA is going directly to cottage municipalities to determine cottages that have been sold and then tracking the owners to ensure they have reflected the disposition for income tax purposes. Others think the CRA is just following up reported dispositions of cottages on personal income tax returns. In either event, we have seen several information requests/audits for clients.

So once the CRA decides to review your cottage sale, what are they looking at and what information are they requesting?

Amongst other things, they are asking you to support the ACB of the property by providing the following:

a) Your copy of the original purchase agreement stating the purchase price.

b) The statement of adjustments where the purchase of the property involved the services of a lawyer.

c) If the property was either inherited or purchased in a non-arm's-length transaction, indicate the FMV of the property on the date of acquisition and supply documentation to support your figure. If the property was inherited, indicate the date of acquisition.

d) A schedule of all capital additions to the property. The schedule must indicate the nature of the addition or improvement (e.g. new roof), as well as the cost.

For items a) and b), hopefully you still have the original documents to provide to the CRA. Item c) is interesting in that where there was a family sale or inheritance, the CRA is seeking validation of the sale price, and possibly cross-checking to see if the family member reported the sale of the cottage, and in the case of a deceased person, to ensure the terminal income tax return of the deceased reported the value of the cottage at death.

Item d) is where the CRA is zeroing in on; the capital additions, as I noted above, are often not tracked and source documents are often not maintained.

The CRA is also asking for support of the proceeds of disposition, requesting such items as a copy of the accepted offer to purchase, the statement of adjustments, and the full name of the purchaser, in addition to their relationship, if any, to you (relative or otherwise).

They are also asking if, while owned by you, the property was your principal residence for any period of time. This relates to the discussion above on when the gain was larger on your cottage than your house, designating your cottage as your PRE. The CRA will then most likely confirm that you did not sell any other residence during that time period.

Another request, if you elected to report a capital gain on the property in 1994, is for a copy of form *T664*, election to report a capital gain on property held at the end of February 22, 1994, that was filed with your 1994 income tax return. This is interesting since many people have not kept their older tax returns, and I don't think the CRA keeps its returns that far back. I am not sure what the CRA is doing in cases where taxpayers have destroyed their elections.

In conclusion, if you have sold a cottage in the last couple years, make sure you have all your documentation in place should you receive an information request, and if you currently own a cottage, use this roadmap to ensure you have updated your cottage ACB and have a file for any documentation needed to support it.

---

1   *Income Tax Act*, RSC 1985, c 1 (5th Supp), s 40(2)

Chapter 12

Proprietorships, Corporations, Holding Companies and Family Trusts – The Technical Stuff

Advice for Entrepreneurs

One of my readers asked what advice I would provide to an entrepreneur starting a business. I really liked their suggestion. My comments, based on 25 years of observation, are discussed below.

Personal Relationships

In my opinion, the most important issue facing any entrepreneur, either involved in a relationship or married, is their significant other. Starting a business requires a significant time commitment and comes with a large element of risk. If your significant other is not willing to support you both financially and spiritually, either your business or relationship/marriage is doomed. Where there is resistance to starting the venture, or the other person does not have the same risk threshold, they seem to just drain the enthusiasm and energy from the entrepreneur. In my opinion, if there is no buy-in from your significant other, your chances of success are diminished before you start.

Be Honest with Yourself

The first thing you must ask yourself before you commence any business is if you are an entrepreneur by choice or circumstance. If it is by choice, move to the next paragraph. If your reason is circumstance (such as being laid off due to a recession), you must realize that unless you are starting a service industry or similar industry where you have portability of your clients or customers (e.g. you start your own law practice and when the economy picks up, if you are hired by law firm, you can take your clients with you to the new firm), this will potentially be a lifelong commitment. If you cannot make a long-term commitment, do not start your business, as it will most likely be doomed to fail.

Business Plans and Cash Flow Statements

My first suggestion is to walk before you run. Make sure you start slowly and have everything you require in place. To ensure you have everything in place, you need a business plan and cash flow statement.

Developing a business plan forces you to consider all aspects of your new business, from production to marketing; and professional fees you will incur. A business plan acts as an initial road map, and although it will change, it provides initial direction.

In almost all cases, the banks will require a business plan and statement of cash flow. For any new business, the revenue line is an educated guess at best; however, the expenses and cash outlays are fairly pre-dictable, and as such, you will have some cost certainty. Once you know your costs, you know the minimum amount of revenue you will require to pay off your creditors and lenders.

Partners and Employees – Know Your Abilities

Most people are either sales-oriented or business-oriented. If you are strong in both aspects, you have the best of both worlds. Whether you start with a partner or hire an employee later, know your strength. If you are a sales person, hire a good bookkeeper or accountant to help you. If you are the business person, hire a good marketing person, or get advice on how to market your product or service.

Type of Business

If you are developing computer software or apps, you are entering an industry with few barriers to entry, and your costs may be limited to the utilities in your basement. However, if you intend to start a service or manufacturing business, you may have serious barriers to entry and financing issues.

Financing

Whether you are starting a service business or manufacturing business, you will likely require financing. Although you may be able to access some small-business loans (research which loans are available to start-up businesses), financing is often problematic for a start-up business. Even when you can obtain financing, you will almost always require some personal capital. Thus, where possible, you should try to start your business after you have worked a few years and built some capital. If you are lucky enough to attract venture capital, they will want to see that you have significant "skin" in the game. Many young entrepreneurs access family money, either as loans or as equity; however, since many start-up businesses fail, you should ensure that if you borrow or capitalize your business with money from your parents, you do not put their retirement plans in jeopardy.

Where possible, have a line of credit or capital cushion arranged in advance.

Marketing

If you cannot afford to hire a marketing consultant to ensure that you have a market for your product or service, utilize the internet for research and – more importantly – talk to people in the industry. Although some people may view you as the competition and avoid speaking to you, others may have benefited from a mentor when they started and might be willing to speak to you (if you are lucky, they may even be willing to provide some mentorship along the way). Either way, get out there and pound the pavement and speak to people.

Don't Discount Your Services or Product

One of the biggest mistakes I have seen entrepreneurs make is discounting their services or products to get business. The problem with this is that your customers will refer you to their friends as a cheap provider, and you will get referred customers who are only looking for discounted services. This cycle is very hard to break. Sell for a fair price, but don't become known as the person with the "cheap prices" unless you can truly make money in that manner.

Keep Your Books Yourself

This is a bit of an unusual suggestion, but if possible you should initially keep your own books and learn about accounting. You may require a bookkeeper to assist you, but you will always be a better decision maker if you understand your own books. You do not want to be dependent on your bookkeeper.

Watch Your Accounts Receivable

It is imperative that you get in the habit of collecting your accounts receivable on a timely basis. This is important for both cash flow and establishing with your customers that you will not allow them to drag out payments. As you grow, you must print out your accounts receivable listing at least every 30 days, and either follow up yourself or have your office assistant or accounts receivable clerk call to promptly collect overdue accounts.

Give It Time to Grow

Most businesses require three to five years to begin to mature and solidify. Thus, you will need patience and an understanding that you will not be "raking in the cash" for several years.

Your Psyche

Many entrepreneurs, at some point in their business lives, have been perilously close to bankruptcy or have actually had a business go bankrupt. While not always the case, entrepreneurs seem to have nerves of steel (or at least give that impression). You may be able to be successful without those steely nerves, but they would be a good attribute if you start a business, so you can face down the many challenges that will confront your business.

Post Mortem

It has been my experience that when entrepreneurs reflect upon their businesses, almost everyone says that if they had known about the physical toll, long hours, and financial stress they would endure, they would not have started their business.

But that is the wisdom or weariness of age. New entrepreneurs are driven and have boundless energy, and they do succeed in spite of the above-noted risks and stresses. However, it is vitally important to plan and to try to implement or consider many of the factors I have noted above to make the journey a little less bumpy.

Proprietorship or Corporation – What Is the Best for Your (New) Business?

I am often asked by clients whether they should incorporate a new business or start as a proprietorship. A logical follow-up question for those that have already started their business as a proprietorship is when should they convert their proprietorship into a corporation? I will address the first question below and the second later in this chapter.

Corporation – Non-Tax Benefit

The number one non-tax reason to incorporate a business is for creditor-proofing. Generally, a corporation provides creditor protection to its shareholders through its limited liability status, a protection not available to a proprietorship. Where an incorporated business is sued and becomes liable for a successful claim, the only assets exposed to the creditors are the corporate assets, not the shareholders' personal assets.

In order to mitigate the exposure that a potential claim can have on corporate assets, a holding company can be incorporated. See discussion later in the chapter.

The inherent nature of certain businesses leads to the risk of lawsuits, while other business types have limited risk of lawsuits. Thus, one of your first decisions upon starting a business is to determine whether your risk of being sued is high; if so, you should incorporate from day one.

Corporation – the Tax Benefits

There are several substantial income tax benefits associated with incorporation:

1. The Lifetime Capital Gains Exemption

    If you believe that your business has substantial growth potential and may be a desirable acquisition target in the future, it is usually suggested to incorporate. That is because on the sale of the shares of a Qualifying Small Business Corporation ("QSBC"), each shareholder may be entitled to an $800,000 capital gains exemption (indexed for inflation).

    Where you start your business as a proprietorship, it is still possible to convert the proprietorship into a corporation on a tax-free basis and to multiply the capital gains exemption going forward.

2. Income Splitting

    A corporation provides greater income splitting opportunities than a proprietorship. With a corporation, it may be possible to utilize discretionary shares that allow the corporation to stream dividends to particular shareholders (e.g. a spouse) who are in lower marginal income tax brackets than the principal owner-manager, or split the income equally amongst spouses.

    Dividends are paid with after-corporate-tax dollars from the business, whereas salaries (the alternative form of remuneration) are paid with pre-tax dollars and are generally a deductible business expense. The deductibility of a salary by a business is subject to a "reasonability test". In order to deduct a salary from the business' income, it must be considered "reasonable". Unfortunately, there is no defined criteria as to what is considered "reasonable"; however, paying a family member a salary of $50,000/annually who has little or no responsibilities within the business likely does not qualify. With dividends there is no such "reasonability test", so paying a family member a dividend of $50,000 even though she/he may have little or no responsibility within the business is perfectly acceptable. Salaries to family members can be paid in an incorporated business or unincorporated business, but the dividend alternative is unique to a corporation. Sole proprietors cannot pay themselves a salary; they receive draws from the proprietorship.

3. Income Tax Rate

The first $500,000 of active business income earned in a corporation is currently subject to an income tax rate of only 15.5% in Ontario. Since the personal rate on income can be as high as 49%, income earned within a corporation potentially provides a very large income tax deferral, assuming these funds are not required personally for living expenses. This potential 34% deferral of income tax allows you to build your business with pre-tax corporate dollars. It should also be noted that once you take the money from the corporation, in many cases you essentially pay the deferred 34% tax as a dividend.

Corporations – the Fine Print

1. Expenses

The deductions allowed in a proprietorship are similar in nature to the deductions permitted in a corporation.

2. Professional and Compliance Costs and Administrative Burdens

The costs to maintain a corporation are significantly higher than for a proprietorship. There are initial and ongoing legal costs, and annual accounting fees to prepare financial statements and file corporate income tax returns. These costs can be significant in some cases, and can even outweigh some of the tax benefits in certain situations.

In addition, the administrative burdens for a corporation are far greater.

So Why Start as a Proprietorship?

If you do not have legal liability concerns and you cannot avail yourself to the enhanced income splitting opportunities with family members that a corporation may provide, starting as a proprietorship keeps your costs down and reduces your compliance and administrative issues. More importantly, since most people need whatever excess cash their business generates in its early years to live on, there is generally little or no tax benefit from incorporating a business initially. Finally, a proprietorship essentially provides an initial test period to determine the viability of the business, and if there are business losses, the owner(s) can generally deduct these losses against his or her other income.

There is no "one shoe fits all" solution in determining whether to start your business as a sole proprietorship or a corporation; however, the answer should become clearer once you address the issues I have outlined above.

Transferring Your Sole Proprietorship into a Corporation

As discussed above, to minimize costs and test the economic waters, many Canadians start their own business as a sole proprietorship. If your business proves successful, and incorporation makes sense for the reasons discussed above (creditor protection, income splitting, capital gains exemption) you can transfer your business into a corporation. I discuss how to do this below.

How Do I Go from a Sole Proprietorship to a Corporation?

There are specific rollover provisions contained in section 85 of the *Income Tax Act* that allow for you to transfer your sole proprietorship to a corporation on a tax-free basis. Shares of the corporation must be received on the transfer. The rollover is undertaken by filing form *T2057*, election on disposition of property by a taxpayer to a taxable Canadian corporation. Although this is a standard transfer provision, it is fraught with landmines.

The legal and accounting fees to undertake this transaction can be costly depending upon the complexity of the transfer. As such, many people decide to forgo this step, especially when they consider their main proprietorship asset to be personal goodwill (you are the business and without you, it is worthless), as opposed to business goodwill (the portion of the business value that cannot be attributed to business assets such as inventory and equipment, e.g. the value of your business name, customer list, intellectual property, etc.); however, if you ignore filing form *T2057*, you do so at your own risk.

This is because when you transfer your assets and goodwill from your proprietorship to a corporation, you are deemed to have sold or disposed of these assets at their fair market value ("FMV"). In order to avoid this deemed sale, and to ensure you do not create any income or capital gains upon the transfer of these assets, I always suggest filing the tax-free rollover under section 85.

As noted above, I have had clients argue they have no business goodwill and that all their goodwill is personal in nature. While in some cases there may be some validity to this argument, I think it is penny wise and pound foolish to take the risk that the Canada Revenue Agency ("CRA") will deem a large gain on the transfer of your proprietorship goodwill when you can just make the election and eliminate that concern.

Once you have decided to roll over your goodwill to the corporation, it needs to be valued for the purposes of the form *T2057*, which can be a costly exercise. While not recommended, if you will be issued all the shares of the corporation, some accountants may accept a client's estimate of their goodwill for purposes of the election, if it is reasonable and supportable. However, where other family members will become shareholders, a professional valuation is required. For example, if John transfers his proprietorship to a corporation and a valuator determines his shares are worth $500,000, John must be issued special shares worth $500,000 to ensure he has not conferred a benefit on his spouse or children. Once the special shares are issued to John, his spouse, family, and/or trust subscribe for new common shares at $1.

It is important to note that I am glossing over several complex attribution rules here, and you should not consider including any family members in the new corporation until you obtain proper income tax and legal advice. It is crucial to understand the ramifications of either decision, and whether dividends must be paid to you in order to avoid the attribution rules.

Cost and Administrative Considerations

The cost of maintaining an incorporated company is far more expensive than operating a proprietorship. You must file financial statements with the CRA, and the corporate income tax returns are complicated. You require annual legal resolutions, and the administration is far more costly. Thus, I would not recommend the use of a corporation (subject to other factors such as creditor-proofing and the capital gains exemption discussed above) unless you could leave approximately $50,000 (at minimum, but more like $75,000) of taxable income in the corporation after any salary you require.

Proprietors sometimes have difficulty separating their corporate funds from their personal funds, as they are used to taking draws and simply paying tax on their business income. The corporate structure is more formal, and personal drawings must be paid in the form of salary with income tax withheld and/or dividends. Both require filing of government forms (T4/T5).

The income tax benefits of a corporation can be significant; however the transfer of a proprietorship to a corporation is very complex, especially when introducing family members as shareholders. It is thus vital that you engage an accountant and a lawyer to explain all the income tax issues to you before undertaking the transfer.

Creditor-Proofing Corporate Funds

Many an owner-manager of a private corporation is concerned about creditors potentially gaining access to their corporation's cash and investments through real or frivolous lawsuits. The simplest method to protect surplus corporate funds is through the use of a holding company.

The *Income Tax Act* generally permits an owner-manager to transfer the shares of their operating company ("Opco") to a new holding company ("Holdco") without incurring any tax. Following this type of transfer, the owner-manager would own the shares of Holdco, which in turn would own the shares of Opco. With that type of ownership structure in place, Opco and Holdco will typically (subject to meeting certain ownership criteria) be known as "connected corporations".[1]

When corporations are connected, they can typically pay their retained earnings (excess cash and other assets net of liabilities of the corporation) as a dividend from Opco to Holdco on a tax-free basis. This has the effect of removing excess cash and other assets from Opco so that it would no longer be susceptible to future creditors' claims. This can be repeated in the future as Opco accumulates additional retained earnings.

If Opco requires ongoing cash and working capital, the funds received by Holdco could be loaned back to Opco on a secured basis provided a General Security Agreement ("GSA") is registered by a lawyer. It is important to note the dividend first paid by Opco must be physically paid by way of a cash or other asset transfer, and then physically loaned back to Opco by Holdco to ensure that the GSA is valid.

Opco's banker should always be advised in advance that Opco is undertaking a creditor-proofing transaction. Where a bank loan or other debt is present, the GSA will secure the loan, but Holdco would generally still rank behind the bank or other secured creditors as far as payment is concerned.

The structure noted above is simple and effective; however, where the owner-manager or other family members have access to the $800,000 capital gains exemption and may potentially sell shares of the company in the future, this type of creditor-proofing transaction may not be appropriate as the excess cash may put the shares offside. Depending on your family and personal financial situation, it may be possible to creditor-proof Opco, maintain potential access to the capital gains exemption, and provide a means to income split with family members in one fell swoop by utilizing a "freeze" transaction with a family trust. (See Chapter 10 for a discussion on "Estate Freezes".)

Introducing a Family Trust as a Shareholder in a Private Corporation

As noted above, the use of a holding company is a simple way for a private corporation to creditor-proof excess corporate funds. A family trust is an alternative structure to a holding company that can not only achieve creditor-proofing, but may also provide for (a) income splitting with family members; (b) multiple accesses to the $800,000 capital gains exemption; and (c) possibly provide a means to crystallize or "freeze" the income tax liability related to your company's shares at death.

To reflect the potential benefits of utilizing a family trust, I will use the example of Starlet Yohansen, who owns all the common shares of Movie Star Limited ("MSL"). The shares initially cost Starlet $1, and are now worth $3,000,000.

For Starlet to concurrently achieve all the objectives noted above, she would typically "freeze" the value of her common shares in MSL. At the date of the "freeze", Starlet would exchange her common shares for special preferred shares with a value equal to the value of the common shares exchanged (that being $3,000,000). Thus, at this point in time, there are no common shares and Starlet owns special shares worth $3,000,000. These special shares cannot increase in value, hence the term "freeze".

Any future growth in the value of MSL over the current value of $3,000,000 will accrue only to the new common shares that are issued as part of this reorganization. That growth will accrue directly, or indirectly through a family trust, to potentially Starlet's family members and/or a holding company by having them subscribe for the new common shares issued in MSL (Starlet can also maintain some of the future growth if she subscribes for the new common shares, or is included in the family trust). Often we see this strategy being used in succession planning when the owner-manager wishes to transfer ownership of their operating company to the next generation, but this strategy can be used without succession being the objective.

The beauty of the freeze is that Starlet's maximum income tax liability on her MSL shares has been established (unless she subscribes for more common shares). At Starlet's death, her income tax liability on her MSL shares will be equal to $3,000,000 x the applicable income tax rate at that time (likely around 23%). As Starlet knows the maximum income tax liability on her special shares, she can plan to pay this liability by putting aside funds or by purchasing life insurance.

In addition, Starlet's future income tax liability can be reduced by redeeming her frozen shares over time, which typically creates a current taxable dividend to Starlet, but also serves to reduce the value of the frozen shares by the amount of the dividend.

If Starlet uses her family trust to subscribe for the new common shares of MSL, the beneficiaries of the family trust would typically include Starlet, her spouse, her children, and a holding company. The inclusion of these beneficiaries can provide tax-effective income splitting on dividends received from MSL when the children are 18 years of age or older, or when a spouse is in a lower income tax bracket (Starlet may have a trophy husband who does not have much income). The trust can also provide tax-effective income splitting on the sale of a business, regardless of the beneficiaries' age.

Generally, a family trust is discretionary. The trustees can tax-effectively allocate the income received by the trust (i.e. dividends from MSL) to any or all of the beneficiaries (including Starlet), so long as they are 18 years of age or older. A beneficiary who is 18 years of age or older and has no other sources of income can receive approximately $40,000 in dividends tax-free. This strategy is a great way to help fund a child's post-secondary education (in addition to a Registered Education Savings Plan ["RESP"]) or other expenses, while also lessening the family's overall income tax liability.

If the shares of MSL are sold in the future, any sale proceeds in excess of the value of Starlet's original frozen special preferred shares ($3,000,000 maximum) can be allocated to the beneficiaries of the trust. This may permit the utilization of the $800,000 capital gains exemption by each of these beneficiaries. A word to the wise though, any sales proceeds allocated to a beneficiary of the trust, including a minor child, will result in the money legally belonging to them.

Finally, back to the original creditor-proofing issue. The inclusion of a holdco as a beneficiary of the trust would provide a means to transfer any excess funds in MSL as tax-free via a dividend from MSL to Holdco, thus creditor-proofing the excess cash in MSL by moving it to Holdco, and keeping the shares eligible for the capital gains exemption.

There are several pitfalls along the way (and in the future) that must be avoided in order to successfully achieve the objectives noted at the beginning of this post. If you are contemplating undertaking such a transaction, you must consult your accountant and lawyer to ensure that the transaction makes sense given your personal situation, and that no details are missed in carrying out the finer points of the reorganization.

Business and Income Tax Issues in Selling a Corporation

The sale of your business/corporation is typically a once-in-a-lifetime event. Thus, in most cases, you will never have experienced the anxiety, manic ups and downs, legal and income tax issues, negotiating stances, walk-away threats, and all the other fun that comes with the experience.

In order to navigate the sale minefield and to come up with a fairly negotiated deal, you will require a team that includes a strong lawyer, accountant, and maybe even a mergers and acquisitions consultant.

With all that to look forward to, I figured I would provide some of the meat-and-potatoes issues you will also have to solve and negotiate.

Assets vs. Shares

In general, the sale of shares will yield a better return for the seller than the sale of assets, especially if the vendor has their $800,000 QSBC capital gains exemptions available. However, the purchaser in most cases will prefer to purchase the assets and goodwill of a business for the following two reasons:

1. The purchaser can depreciate assets and amortize goodwill for income tax purposes, whereas the cost of a share purchase is allocated to the cost base of the shares.

2. The purchaser does not assume any legal liability of the vendor when they purchase assets and goodwill, whereas under a share purchase agreement, the purchaser becomes liable for any past sins of the acquired corporation (of course, the purchaser's lawyer will covenant away most of these issues as best they can).

Consequently, the purchaser typically wishes to buy assets, whereas the seller wishes to sell shares, and thus the first negotiation point. Whichever way it goes, the buyer knows why you want to sell shares, and will typically discount the offer when buying shares instead of assets.

Working Capital

Working Capital ("WC") is the difference between current assets and current liabilities, and measures the liquidity of a company. In simple terms, WC is cash plus accounts receivable and inventory less accounts payable. WC can be a huge bone of contention in any sale, but especially in an asset sale. In most cases the seller blissfully assumes they will keep all the WC, and also get a multiple of the corporation's earnings as the sale price. The purchaser typically wants enough WC left in the business such that they will not need to finance the business once they have made the initial purchase and contributed whatever cash or line of credit they feel is required upon the initial purchase.

The WC is a very esoteric concept at best, and very hard for most sellers to grasp. Thus, it is vital to deal with this issue upfront and not leave it to the end where it can derail a deal – something I have experienced firsthand.

Valuation

Most sellers have valuation multiples dancing around in their heads like little sugar plum fairies; however, most industries have standard valuation multiples. For most small businesses, the multiple is somewhere between two to four times earnings, with a higher multiple for strategic acquisitions (especially where the purchaser is a public company, since they themselves may have a 15 to 20 multiple).

For many acquisitions, especially by public and larger corporations, the multiple is based on earnings before interest, taxes and amortization ("EBITA"). However, in addition to EBITA, there will be adjustments to the upside for management salaries in excess of the salary that would be required to replace the current owner (typically you are adding back bonuses paid to the seller in excess of their monthly wages and any other family wages). Occasionally, the adjustment can be to the downside, but that is typically only in situations where the business is a technology company (or similar) that is just starting to make money or finalize a desired product, and the owner's wages have not yet caught up to market value. Finally, there will be other additions to EBITA for things like car expenses, advertising and promotion, etc., that a new owner would not necessarily need to incur upon the sale.

Where a purchase is made by a private company, the price may be based on a capitalization of normalized after-tax earnings or discretionary cash flows instead of EBITA.

Retention

In most cases, the purchaser will require the seller to stay on for a year or two to ensure a smooth transition. The owner will thus be entitled to a salary for that period in addition to the sales proceeds. The retention period can go several ways: some blow up quickly, some end after the year or two, but often the former owner stays on (as the business is now growing due to additional funds or more sophisticated management, and they enjoy remaining with their baby without the stress of ownership).

Continued Ownership

It is not uncommon for a purchaser to require that the seller maintain some ownership in their company so that they still have some "skin" in the game, especially when they will be staying on with the business. This is also the case where the purchaser is consolidating several similar businesses with the intent of going public. In these cases, I counsel my clients to assume the worst (e.g. that the new owner will make a mess of the business), and ensure they receive proceeds equal to (or only slightly less than) what they initially desired. I have seen several disasters in consolidation purchases where the seller ended up with minimal proceeds after keeping significant share positions due to the lure of the consolidated entity going public, and the consolidated company just did not have the expected synergies.

Tax Reorganizations

Where the deal is a share purchase, often the current corporate structure is not conducive to utilizing the QSBC capital gains exemption, especially where a holding company is in place or the company being sold has a large cash position. It is thus vital to ensure at least some initial income tax planning is done so that if the deal moves forward, proper consideration has been given to the income tax planning, and the planning is not a wild, last minute scramble.

I have only touched on a few of the multitude of issues you may encounter upon the sale of your business. As noted initially, it is vital to understand the process and how stressful it may be from the start, and to assemble the proper team to help you navigate through the sale process.

---

1 *Income Tax Act*, RSC 1985, c 1 (5th Supp), s 256(1)

Acknowledgements

A successful blog takes on a life of its own and can, at times, be all-consuming. Several people have been instrumental along the way and I would like to acknowledge their contributions. First, I would like to thank my wife Lori, for her unwavering support and understanding. I have spent many a weekend pounding the keyboard instead of spending quality time with her or helping around the house. Lori has also served as my sounding board, ensuring that I use "plain English" to make my blog posts more readable.

I would also like to thank Cunningham LLP's former marketing manager, Lisa Cutler. She set up *The Blunt Bean Counter*'s framework and was a great first editor of my posts.

Finally, I'm very appreciative of Lynda Kremer's efforts. She is Cunningham's Marketing Coordinator and has truly been invaluable in putting this book together.

CPSIA information can be obtained at www.ICGtesting.com
Printed in the USA
LVOW07s1551151015

458413LV00015B/940/P